SOUL IDOLATRY

EXCLUDES MEN OUT OF HEAVEN

SOUL

IDOLATRY

Excludes Men

Out of Heaven

BY

David Clarkson

Published by

CURIOSMITH

Minneapolis

2010

NOTES FROM THE PUBLISHER

1. The "Guide to the Contents" was added to this edition by the publisher.
2. Isaiah 31:11, page 18, does not exist, no replacement found.
3. Isaiah 36:37, page 58, does not exist, no replacement found.
4. John 4:28, page 81, subject matched better with John 4:23.
5. 1 Corinthians 13:15, page 85, does not exist, subject matched with
   1 Corinthians 3:15.

Published by Curiosmith.
P. O. Box 390293, Minneapolis, Minnesota, 55439.
Internet: curiosmith.com.
E-mail: shopkeeper@curiosmith.com.

Reprinted from:
The Works of David Clarkson, published by James Nichol in 1864.

ISBN 9781935626169

GUIDE TO THE CONTENTS

——◆◆——

SOUL IDOLATRY EXCLUDES
MEN OUT OF HEAVEN

For this ye know, that no whoremonger, nor unclean person, nor covetous man, who is an idolater, hath any inheritance in the kingdom of Christ and of God.—Ephesians 5:5.

THE apostle, in the former chapter, and the beginning of this, we find exhorting the Ephesians to holy walking. He proceeds herein positively, verses 1, 2. The argument is, 'Hereby ye shall be followers of God.' Ye are his children, dear to him upon many accounts; and it becomes children to follow, to imitate their father; to follow him, though it be not *passibus æquis;* to follow him at a distance, though ye cannot come up to him: verse 2, 'Walk in love.' The argument drawn from the love of Christ, the most forcible argument to a member of Christ: 'The love of Christ should constrain,' etc. It answers all objections. How? Love those that hate, revile, disparage, etc. Christ died for enemies. Walk in love, Christ died in love. To die is more than to walk.

2. Negatively: verse 3, the argument, 'It becometh saints.' Those that are separated to God

as his in peculiar, should be so far separated from these pollutions as they should not name them, but as they name that which is shameful and abominable. They should be so far from committing them, as they should not mention them without detestation.

Verse 4. He extends it not only to their actions, but to their words; not only worldly, filthy, blasphemous talking should be avoided, but 'foolish talking,' that discourse which is vain, idle, unedifying; not only that which is foolish, but that which is counted witty. Scurrilous, abusive wit is not convenient for saints. He uses that very word, ἐυτραπελία, by which Aristotle expresses one of his moral virtues. By which we may perceive the dimness of the light of nature in those who saw clearest. Those that have no better guide may mistake a vice for a virtue.

He adds the reason, verse 5; argues *a concessis*, 'This ye know;' a covetous man, and the like may be understood of the rest, is an idolater, and no idolater hath any inheritance, etc.

Not only the covetous, but the unclean, are idolaters; for the apostle, who here makes covetousness to be idolatry, counts voluptuous persons idolaters also, where he speaks of some who make their belly their God, Philippians 3. Indeed, every reigning lust is an idol, and every person in whom it reigns is an idolater. 'The lust of the flesh, the lust of the eye, and the pride of life,' *i. e.* pleasures, and riches, and honours, are the carnal man's trinity, the three great idols of worldly men, to which they prostrate their souls; and giving that to them which is due only to God, they hereby become guilty of idolatry, according to that remarkable speech of Cyprian, (*Serm. de jejun. et tent.*) *Diaboli in regno genu flexo concupiscentiæ suæ idolum quisque colit.* In Satan's kingdom, every one bowing himself to his lust worships it as an idol. That this may be more evident, that covetousness, uncleaness, and other lusts are idolatry, let us consider what it is, and the several kinds of it. Idolatry is το λατρεύειν τῇ κτισει παρὰ τὸν κτίσαντα, Romans 1:25, to give that honour and worship to the creature which is due only to God. Or as Nazianzen, Orat. 33, μετάθεσις τῆς πρόσκυνήσεως ἀπο τοῦ πεποιηκότος ἐπι τα κτισμάτα, to transfer that respect which is due only to God, from him to the creature. There is some honour, some worship, which is proper to God alone, Isaiah 42:8, Matthew 4:10, Isaiah 45:23. Now when this worship is made common, communicated to other things, whatever they are, we hereby make them idols, and commit idolatry. Now this worship due to God only is not only given by heathens to their false gods, and by papists to angels, saints, images, etc., but also by carnal men to their lusts. For there is a twofold worship (as all agree) due only to God, internal and external.

1. External, which consists in acts and gestures of the body. When a man bows to, or prostrates himself before, a thing, this is the worship of the body; and when these gestures of bowing,

prostration are used, not out of a civil, but a religious respect, with an intention to testify divine honour, then it is worship due only to God.

2. Internal, which consists in the acts of the soul and actions answerable thereto. When the mind is most taken up with an object, and the heart and affections most set upon it, this is soul worship, and this is due only to God. For he being the chief good, and the last end of intelligent creatures, it is his due, proper to him alone, to be most minded and most affected; it is the honour due only to the Lord to have the first, the highest place, both in our minds and hearts and endeavours.

Now according to this distinction of worship there are two sorts of idolatry,

1. Open, outward idolatry, when men, out of a religious respect, bow to or prostrate themselves before anything besides God. This is the idolatry of the heathens, and part of the idolatry of papists.

2. Secret and soul idolatry, when the mind and heart is set upon anything more than God; when anything is more valued, more intended; anything more trusted, more loved, or our endeavours more for any other thing than God. Then is that soul worship, which is due only to God (and that which he most respects and calls for) given to other things besides him. And this is as true, as heinous idolatry, as the former, though not so open, discernible, nor so much observed.

And it is this secret, this soul idolatry which

the apostle intends, when he calls voluptuous men idolaters, Philippians 3; and when he calls covetousness idolatry, Colossians 3:5; and when he styles unclean, covetous persons idolaters in the text. Hence,

Observation. Secret idolaters shall have no inheritance in the kingdom of God. Soul idolatry will exclude men out of heaven as well as open idolatry. He that serves his lusts is as uncapable of heaven as he that serves, worships idols of wood or stone.

Before we come to confirm and apply this truth, it will be requisite to make a more clear discovery of this secret idolatry, the most that are guilty of it not taking notice of their guilt, because they account nothing idolatry but what is openly and outwardly so. In order thereunto, observe, there are thirteen acts of soul worship; and to give any one of them to anything besides the God of heaven is plain idolatry, and those idolaters that so give it.

1. *Esteem.* That which we most highly value we make our God. For estimation is an act of soul worship. *Cultus et veneratio denotant præcipue internam rei excellentis æstimationem*, worship is the mind's esteem of a thing as most excellent. Now the Lord challenges the highest esteem, as an act of honour and worship due only to himself. Therefore to have an high esteem of other things, when we have low thoughts of God, is idolatry. To have an high opinion of ourselves, of our parts and accomplishments, of our relations

and enjoyments, of riches and honours, or those that are rich and honourable, or anything of like nature, when we have low apprehensions of God, is to advance these things into the place of God; to make them idols, and give them that honour and worship which is due only to the divine Majesty. What we most esteem we make our god; if other things are of higher esteem, ye are idolaters, Job 21:14.

2. *Mindfulness.* That which we are most mindful of we make our God. To be most remembered, to be most minded, is an act of worship which is proper to God, and which he requires as due to himself alone, Ecclesiastes 12:1. Other things may be minded; but if they be more minded than God, it is idolatry, the worship of God is given to the creature. When ye mind yourselves, mind your estates and interests, mind your profits or pleasures more than God, you set these up as idols in the place of God; when that time, which should be taken up with thoughts of God, is spent in thoughts of other things; when God is not in all your thoughts, or if he sometimes be there, yet if other things take place of him in your thoughts; if when ye are called to think of God (as sometimes every day we should do with all seriousness), if ordinarily and willingly you make these thoughts of God give place to other things, it is idolatry.

If either you do not think of God, or think otherwise of him than he is: think him all mercy, not minding his justice; think him all pity and compassion, not minding his purity and holiness; think of his faithfulness in performing promises, not at all minding his truth in execution of threatenings; think him all love, not regarding his sovereignty: this is to set up an idol instead of God. Thinking otherwise of God than he has revealed himself, or minding other things as much or more than God, is idolatry.

3. *Intention.* That which we most intend we make our god; for to be most intended is an act of worship due only to the true God; for he being the chief good must be the last end. Now the last end must be our chief aim, *i. e.* it must be intended and aimed at for itself; and all other things must be aimed at for its sake, in a reference, in a subserviency to it.

Now, when we make other things our chief aim, or main design, we set them up in the stead of God, and make them idols; when our chief design is to be rich, or great, or safe, or famous, or powerful; when our great aim is our own ease, or pleasure, or credit, or profit and advantage; when we aim at, or intend any [thing] more, or anything so much, as the glorifying and enjoying of God: this is soul idolatry. And oh, if men would impartially search their hearts, and examine their intentions, how much idolatry might they discover, which is not now taken notice of!

4. *Resolution.* What we are most resolved for we worship as God. Resolvedness for God, above all things, is an act of worship which he challenges as due to himself alone. To communicate

it to other things, is to give the worship of God unto them, and so to make them gods. When we are fully resolved for other things, for our lusts, humours, outward advantages, and but faintly resolved for God, his ways, honour, service;

When we resolve absolutely for other things without limitation or restriction, and but conditionally for God, upon such and such terms; to serve him, so as ye may serve yourselves too; to seek him so as to enjoy your lusts with him;

When resolve presently for other things, but refer our resolves for God to the future; let me get enough of the world, of my pleasure, of my lusts, now; I will think of God hereafter, in old age, in sickness, on a death-bed: these are idolatrous resolutions; God is thrust down, the creatures and your lusts advanced into the place of God; and that honour which is due only to him you give unto them. This is unquestionable idolatry.

5. *Love*. That which we must love we worship as our God; for love is an act of soul-worship, *idem est*, προσκυνεῖν κὰι φιλεῖν. To love and to adore are sometimes both one. *Quod quis amat, id etiam adorat*, that which one loves he worships. This is undoubtedly true, if we intend hereby that love which is superlative and transcendent; for to be loved above all things is an act of honour, worship, which the Lord challenges as his due in peculiar, Deuteronomy 6:5. In this the Lord Christ comprised all that worship which is required of man, Matthew 22:37. Other things may be loved, but he will be loved above all other

things. He is to be loved transcendently, absolutely, and for himself; all other things are to be
loved in him and for him. He looks upon us as
not worshipping him at all, not taking him for a
God, when we love other things more, or as much
as himself, 1 John 2:15. Those that are φιλήδονοι
μᾶλλον ἢ φιλοθεοι, 'lovers of pleasures,' 2 Timothy
3:4, they make their pleasures, their bellies, their
god, Philippians 3:19; those that love their riches,
the things of the world, more than, or equally
with, God, they make these their gods, worship a
golden calf: this is the idol in the text. Those that
love their relations, etc., Matthew 10:37, Luke
14:26, those that love themselves more than God,
idolise themselves. Love, whenever it is inordinate, it is an idolatrous affection.

6. *Trust.* That which we most trust we make
our god; for confidence and dependence is an act
of worship which the Lord calls for as due only to
himself. And what act of worship is there which
the Lord more requires, than this soul-depen-
dence upon him alone? Proverbs 3:5, 'With all
thy heart.' He will have no place there left for
confidence in anything else; therefore, it is idolatry to trust in ourselves, to rely upon our own
wisdom, judgments, parts, accomplishments; the
Lord forbids it, Proverbs 3:5.

To trust in means or instruments. The church
disclaims this, Psalm 20:7; as also Psalm 44:6,
'I will not trust in my bow.' Asa is branded for
dependence on physicians, 2 Chronicles 16:12.

To trust in wealth or riches. Job disclaims

this, and reckons it amongst those idolatrous acts that were punishable by the judge, Job 31:24. David joins this and the disclaiming of God together, Psalm 52:7; and our apostle, who calls covetousness idolatry, dissuades from this confidence in riches, as inconsistent with confidence in God, 1 Timothy 6:17.

To trust in friends, though many and mighty, Jeremiah 17:5. He fixes a curse upon this, as being a departing from, a renouncing of, God; an advancing of that we trust in to the room of God, Psalm 146:3. These are such idols, when trusted, as those who have eyes, etc.; hence, Psalm 118:8–9, 'Better to trust,' etc. As in the mighty, so in the many, Hosea 10:13. Idols are called lies in Scripture; such are these, etc., Isaiah 31:11. The idolatry of this confidence is expressed, in that the true God is laid aside. Trust in the creature is always idolatrous.

7. *Fear*. That which we most fear we worship as our god; for fear is an act of worship, *est adoratio quæ timorem significat* (Thurasus Nicen. 2). He that does fear, does worship that which is feared, which is unquestionable when his fear is transcendent. The whole worship of God is frequently in Scripture expressed by this one word *fear*, Matthew 4:10, and Deuteronomy 6:13; and the Lord challenges this worship, this fear, as due to him alone, Isaiah 51:12, 19. That is our god which is our fear and dread, Luke 12:4–5. If you fear others more than him, you give that worship to them which is due only to God; and

this is plain idolatry; hence the fearful are reckoned amongst idolaters, and the same sentence
denounced against them as against idolatry, in
the text, Revelation 21:8. Those, therefore, who
fear other things more than God; who are more
afraid to offend men than to displease God; who
fear more to lose any outward enjoyment, than
to lose the favour of God; who fear outward sufferings more than God's displeasure; who had
rather sin than suffer; more afraid of troubles in
the world, than of losing peace with God; those
whom the sight of man will more restrain from
sin than the all-seeing eye of God; who will venture to make more bold with God than men, and
stand in more awe of others than God: they stand
guilty of idolatry, that which is here threatened.

8. *Hope.* That which we make our hope we
worship as God; for hope is an act of worship;
qui sperat, adorat, that which we make our hope
we worship, and worship is due only to God. It
is his prerogative to be the hope of his people,
Jeremiah 17:13, Romans 15:13. When we make
other things our hope, we give them the honour
due only to God; it is a forsaking of the Lord
the fountain, and advancing of broken cisterns
into his place, hereby worshipping them as God
only should be worshipped. Thus do the papists
openly, when they call the virgin mother, the
wooden cross, and saints departed, their hope;
and thus do others amongst us, who make their
prayers, their sorrow for sin, their works of
charity, or any acts of religion or righteousness,

their hope; when men expect hereby to satisfy justice, to pacify God's displeasure, to procure heaven. Nothing can effect this, but that which is infinite, the righteousness of God; and this we having only in and from Christ, he is therefore called our hope, 1 Timothy 1:1; 'our hope of glory,' Colossians 1:27. Those that make their own righteousness the foundation of their hope, they exalt it into the place of Christ, and honour it as God; and to honour anything as God, is evident idolatry.

And so it is, not only in expectation of eternal glory, but outward happiness. When our principal hope is in friends, riches, etc., it is idolatry; for this is to worship them instead of God. And Job ranks it with that gross idolatry of worshipping the sun or moon, Job 31:24, 29.

9. *Desire.* That which we most desire we worship as our god; for that which is chiefly desired, is the chief good in his account who so desires it; and what he counts his chief good, that he makes his god. Desire is an act of worship; *Est adoratio quæ desiderium significat*, that we most adore which we most desire; and to be most desired is that worship, that honour, which is due only to God. To desire anything more, or so much as the enjoyment of God, is to idolise it, to prostrate the heart to it, and worship it as God only should be worshipped. He only should be that one thing desirable to us above all things, as to David, Psalm 27:4. Those that desire corn, and wine, and oil, more than the light of God's

countenance, the favour of great men more than the sense of God's love, and to live in mirth and jollity, in abundance of worldly enjoyments, rather than holily in spiritual communion with God; to be rich in the world, rather than to be rich towards God; those that desire anything in heaven or earth, as much or more than they desire God, are idolaters, such as the apostle threatens.

10. *Delight.* That which we most delight and rejoice in, that we worship as God; for transcendent delight is an act of worship due only to God; and this affection, in its height and elevation, is called glorying. That which is our delight above all things we glory in it; and this is the prerogative which the Lord challenges, 1 Corinthians 1:31, Jeremiah 9:23–24. To rejoice more in our wisdom, strength, riches, than in the Lord, is to idolize them. To take more delight in relations, wife, or children, in outward comforts and accommodations, than in God, is to worship them, as we ought only to worship God. To take more pleasure in any way of sin, uncleanness, intemperance, earthly employments, than in the holy ways of God, than in those spiritual and heavenly services wherein we may enjoy God, is idolatry. Thus those who take most pleasure in drinking or eating, make their bellies their god; and those who most delight in fulfilling their lusts, be it a worldly, or an unclean, or a revengeful lust, they exalt their lusts above the God of heaven, and worship them; and this is a more

heinous idolatry than to fall down and worship the sun or moon, angels or saints, because these are more worthy of honour than base lusts; nay, it is worse than to worship the devil, since Satan himself, being a creature, is not so vile as the lusts of men. And yet this is the common sin of unregenerate men, and the whole world of them lies in this idolatry, worshipping not only the creature, but their base lusts, before the God of glory.

11. *Zeal.* That for which we are more zealous we worship as god; for such a zeal is an act of worship due only to God; therefore it is idolatrous to be more zealous for our own things than for the things of God; to be eager in our own cause, and careless in the cause of God; to be more vehement for our own credit, interests, advantages, than for the truths, ways, honour of God; to be fervent in spirit, in following our own business, promoting our designs, but lukewarm and indifferent in the service of God; to count it intolerable for ourselves to be reproached, slandered, reviled, but manifest no indignation when God is dishonoured, his name, Sabbaths, worship, profaned; his truths, ways, people, reviled. This is idolatrous; for it shews something is dearer to us than God; and whatever that be, it is an idol; and thy zeal for it is thy worshipping of it, even with that worship which is due only to God.

12. *Gratitude.* That to which we are most grateful, that we worship as God; for gratitude is an act of worship, *est adoratio quæ gratiam notat.*

We worship that to which we are most thankful. We may be thankful to men, we may acknowledge the helplessness of means and instruments; but if we rest here, and rise not higher in our thanks and acknowledgments; if the Lord be not remembered as him, without whom all these are nothing: it is idolatry. For this the Lord menaces those idolaters, Hosea 2:5, 8. Thus when we ascribe our plenty, riches, to our care, industry; our success to our prudence, diligence; our deliverances to friends, means, instruments, without looking higher, or not so much to God as unto these, we idolize them, sacrifice to them, as the prophet expresses it, Habakkuk 1:16. To ascribe that which comes from God unto the creatures, is to set them in the place of God, and so to worship them.

Thus you see wherein this secret idolatry consists, and how many ways we may be guilty of it. Many more might be found out, but I shall but add this one. Then we are guilty of this idolatry,

13. When our *care and industry* is more for other things than for God. No man can serve two masters. We cannot serve God and mammon, God and our lusts too, because this service of ourselves, of the world, takes up that care, that industry, those endeavours, which the Lord must have of necessity, if we will serve him as God; and when these are laid out upon the world and our lusts, we serve them as the Lord ought to be served, and so make them our gods. When you are more careful and industrious to please men,

or yourselves, than to please God; to provide for yourselves and posterity, than to be serviceable unto God; more careful what you shall eat, drink, or wherewith be clothed, than how you may honour and enjoy God; to make provision for the flesh, to fulfil the lusts thereof, than how to fulfil the will of God; more industrious to promote your own interests, than the designs of God; to be rich, or great, or respected amongst men, than that God may be honoured and advanced in the world; more careful how to get the things of the world, than how to employ them for God; rise early, go to bed late, eat the bread of carefulness, that your outward estate may prosper, while the cause, and ways, and interests of Christ have few or none of your endeavours, this is to idolize the world, yourselves, your lusts, your relations, while the God of heaven is neglected, and the worship and service due unto him alone is hereby idolatrously given to other things.

Argument 1. Such idolaters are not in covenant with God. It is the covenant of grace alone which gives right and title to the kingdom. Those that are not in covenant, have no title to heaven; and those that have no right nor title to it, shall have no inheritance in it. They are not in covenant; for the very first article of the covenant is, that we take the Lord for our God, and that we have no other gods but him. But idolaters have many other gods. Their hearts never subscribed the covenant of grace; they are in league with other gods, with the world, the flesh, their lusts.

No entering into covenant but by renouncing of these. Till then, ye are in covenant with hell and death; no title to the inheritance, no hopes of it.

2. Such idolaters are not yet born again, are not yet converted; and without the new birth, no inheritance in the kingdom; those only are heirs of this kingdom, who are born of God, who are born again. The Lord Christ affirms this twice together, to make it sure, and affirms it with a double asseveration, John 3:3, 5. No receiving this inheritance till conversion, till turned from darkness, from the power of Satan, who engages all his power to continue sinners in the service of other gods, Acts 26:18. No entering the kingdom except ye be converted, Matthew 18:3. Now conversion is, the apostle tells us, 1 Thessalonians 1:9, 'a turning from idols;' not only from those with which men commit open, but secret idolatry. Till the heart be turned from idols, till this secret idolatry be renounced, there is no conversion; and without this no salvation, no inheritance in the kingdom of God, etc.

Use 1. *Information*. This shews us the misery of a great part of the world; nay, of the greatest part of Christians; nay, of many of them who have escaped the gross idolatry of pagans, or apostate Christians. Not only open, but secret idolatry, excludes from any inheritance in the kingdom of heaven; and this secret idolatry is so common, as the disciples' question will not be unseasonable. Alas! 'Then who shall be saved?' Where is that heart in which some idol is not secretly advanced? Where is that soul that does not bow down to some lust or vanity? Where is that man that does not give that soul-worship to the creature which is due unto the Creator? Some there are, indeed, though few, that are not defiled with this idolatry; but they are none of this number who are yet in the state of nature. Every natural man, let his enjoyments, privileges, accomplishments, be what they will, is an idolater. He that is not converted, changed, born again; he that lives in any known sin, be it uncleanness, or covetousness, or pride, besides the visible guilt of these gross sins, he is a secret idolater; and no idolater shall have any inheritance in the kingdom of God.

Question. Whether may the regenerate be guilty of this secret idolatry? Whether may those who are truly sanctified give this soul-worship to other things, which is due only to God? It seems difficult to determine this either way, the reasons being weighty for both, affirmative and negative; for,

If it be denied, what shall we say to those many instances which Scripture affords, whereby it is too evident that the people of God may fall into incest, drunkenness, murder, adultery, denying of Christ, nay, idolatry itself? Solomon is a sad example hereof, yet he a chosen vessel. The name *Jedidiah*, given him by the Lord, tells us he was beloved of God; yet he, 1 Kings 11:7–8, etc.

But if it be granted on the other side, other difficulties occur; for how can this be consistent with the state of grace, since the sincerity of that state consists in this very point, that the interest of God be advanced in the soul above all other interests? Besides, this is a plain breach of the contract with Christ, for secret idolatry is spiritual adultery. It passes under this name ordinarily in Scripture. Other failings a husband may endure in his wife; but such unfaithfulness tends to dissolve the conjugal covenant. And this in the text is not the least difficulty: for how can they retain a title to the inheritance under this guilt, since the apostle is peremptory, such shall not inherit the kingdom? etc.

Answer. Take the resolution of this difficulty in these three conclusions:

1. There is an aptness and propenseness, in those that are sanctified, to this idolatry as to other sins. Man's corrupt nature is the nursery, the seed-plot of every sin, and this amongst the rest. The fruit of our first sin in Adam is the corruption of our natures, which consists in a proneness, a disposedness, to all abominations, idolatry not excepted. Grace being imperfect in this life, does but correct this corruption in part, it does not extinguish it; it weakens this disposition to idolatry, it does not abolish it. Those natures that are most sanctified on earth are still a seminary of sin; there is in them the roots, the seeds of atheism, blasphemy, murder, adultery, apostasy, and idolatry. Though the virtue of these roots of bitterness be weakened by renewing grace, yet it is not quite lost; the old man abides in those

that are most renewed, and it is furnished with all its members; though they may be weakened, maimed, mortified, yet not one of them is quite perished. And what these members are, the apostle gives us an account, and reckons this very idolatry amongst the rest, Colossians 3:5. He writes to those that were sanctified, and yet he speaks of this and the rest as their members: 'Mortify your,' etc. This is a member of the body of death, which has place in the most sanctified heart on earth; though it be mortified in them, yet is not annihilated. This disposedness to idolatry remains more or less in the best, while the body of death remains; and this we part not with till the soul part from the body.

This is idolatry *in semine*, in the seed and root of it, the proneness of our depraved natures to it. We may call it virtual idolatry; and of this the regenerate are guilty, and will have cause, while they live, to bewail their guilt.

2. They may be guilty of idolatrous acts and motions. This proneness and disposedness to idolatry may come into act; this root of bitterness may sprout and bud; this seed of idolatry in their natures may fructify, and bring forth too much of this cursed fruit; this member of the body of death may act and move. The old man is not dead in those that are sanctified, though it be dying, and while it is alive, it will move, it will be in action more or less, some time or other. And that the saints may be guilty herein, the reason is here evident. The apostle calls covetousness

idolatry here; and voluptuousness idolatry, Philippians 3; so far therefore as any be guilty of covetousness, etc., so far they may be tainted with idolatry. But the regenerate may be guilty of covetousness, not only in respect of proneness and disposedness to it, but actually; chargeable with covetous acts and motions, and therefore with idolatrous acts and motions.

And if in this particular, so in the rest formerly specified; for wherein does the idolatry of covetousness consist, but in this? That it is an inordinate, an immoderate love of riches. Now if love in the renewed may be inordinate, so may other affections, desire, delight, zeal, fear, sorrow; there is like reason for all. And if there may be inordinacy in these motions of the will, there may be the like in the acts of the mind. And therefore the regenerate may be guilty of idolatrous acts and motions, both in mind and heart.

3. They are not guilty of habitual idolatry, as unrenewed men are. The Lord has the habitual pre-eminence in their hearts, when other interests are actually advanced, as a king may keep his throne; when rebels may prevail in part of his dominions.

They are not habitual idolaters. They yield not [to] these idolatrous motions knowingly, willingly, constantly, as others do; they are not tolerated, allowed; they are not unresisted, unlamented; they offer not themselves thereto, but are surprised by them; they are against the constant bent of their hearts, against, purposes and resolutions, against prayers and endeavours.

When they discover these motions, they are astonished at them. They loathe and abhor, they judge and condemn themselves for them; they bewail and lament them, they are their grief and soul affliction; they fly to the blood of Christ for pardon, to the power of Christ for strength against them, and are diligent in the use of mortifying duties to get them subdued; they cry to the Lord with strong cries, as the ravished virgin was to cry out, to shew it is not by consent, but violence, that these prevail. There is a resistance, not only from conscience, but the will, even when it too far consents.

So that these inordinate motions, though idolatrous, are not the idolatry of natural unrenewed men; it is not reigning habitual idolatry. And so the difficulties objected are overcome; for it is this reigning habitual idolatry (not that which is virtual, not that which consists in some inordinate acts and motions resisted, bewailed, pardoned) which is inconsistent with sincerity of grace, which is that spiritual whoredom with which a covenant with Christ cannot consist, which excludes from the inheritance of the kingdom. Of this the regenerate are not guilty; with the two former they may be tainted.

Use 2. *Examination.* Try whether you be guilty of this soul idolatry or no. Idolatry is (according to its *etymon*) a worshipping of idols. It speaks two things, worship and idols. Therefore, that we may make a full discovery of it, let us inquire both after the objects and the acts; search both what are those idols that are worshipped, and what are those acts of worship that are given to them. And to stir you up to this examination, let me premise these two things, the danger and secrecy of this.

1. The danger. It is a sin will endanger your loss of heaven, make it exceeding difficult, or altogether impossible. If one should tell you of some mischievous person lurking in your house, with an intent to murder you, or set your house on fire, etc. The apostle tells you of something more mischievous; that which is more danger-ous, and nearer to you; that which will endanger the loss of an inheritance, of a kingdom.

2. The secrecy of it calls for diligent search. Nothing more common or more concealed. How common is this soul idolatry in the soul of every unsanctified man! There are chambers of imag-ery (to allude to that in the prophet, Ezekiel 8:12), idols set up in every room, in every faculty of man's soul, which he worships in the dark, in secret; so much in the dark, as others can-not see it, himself will not acknowledge it. None more ready to disclaim it than those who are most guilty; take it for a groundless and injuri-ous slander if any charge them with idolatry. They acknowledge the true God, and have none, worship none but him, whatever pagans and papists do. This is the confidence of most. They know of no idols, are conscious of no idolatry, whereas in every corner of their hearts there are multitudes of idols; and the most acts of their

souls are idolatrous worship of those idols. They are apt to say, as Jacob to Laban of his idols: Genesis 31:32, 'With whomsoever thou findest these gods, let him not live;' whereas they are hid in every man's tent, covered in the stuff, hid so secretly as an ordinary search will not discover them, so as to convince the party of his guilt.

Yet, though few will own it, nothing is more common. And therefore it is necessary something be spoken in order to conviction, that ignorance may not be pretended; that men may come to the knowledge of this sin; that you may see it, be ashamed of it, be humbled for it, see a necessity of Christ his blood to wash away this crimson sin; or if men will not see, they may be left without excuse. Search: 1, idols; 2, worship.

1. Every man in the state of nature makes an idol of himself; exalts himself when he should advance God; minds himself more than he minds God; aims at himself, when he should aim at God: rests in himself, when he should depend upon God; loves himself more than God; honours himself more than God; seeks himself more than God; would have that ascribed to himself, which is to be ascribed only to God; would have himself eyed, admired, praised more than God. Self-conceit, self-love, self-seeking, they are all secret strains of idolatry, and ourselves are naturally our own idols.

Nay, further, he makes every part of himself an idol.

2. He makes his understanding his God, by

preferring his own wisdom before the wisdom of God; making his own judgment his guide, and not the word of God, which infinite Wisdom has prescribed as our rule and guide; quarrelling at providence, as though he knew what is more good, more fit for him than God himself; as though he could dispose things more wisely than infinite wisdom. How ordinary is this, both in respect of public and private dispensations! If I had had the disposing, the ordering of those affairs, of this or that event, it should have been otherwise ordered, it should have gone better with the church, with the state, with myself! So relying upon his own understanding more than the wisdom of God; depending on, and being more confident of, his own projects and contrivements than on the providences of God.

3. He makes his own will his God; idolises it, by preferring his will before the will of God. This ye do when ye will not submit to the will of God in suffering what he inflicts; when ye will not obey the will of God in doing what he commands, in avoiding what he forbids. You hereby set your wills in the place of God's. To instance:

It is God's will you should accept Christ upon his own terms. You will not; you break his bands, etc.; count his burden too heavy, his yoke not easy.

It is God's will you should live holily, according to the rule of the gospel. You will not; you count it too strict, too precise, brand it, etc.

It is his will you set up his worship in your families.

It is his will you avoid swearing, Sabbath-breaking, drunkenness, uncleanness, break off these sins by repentance. You will not. Do ye not evidently herein prefer your wills before the will of God, and thereby idolise them? Here is a double guilt in every such sin, indeed in every known sin; here is both disobedience, not doing the will of God, and idolatry, preferring your own will before his. Such rebellion is as the sin of witchcraft; such stubbornness is as iniquity and idolatry, as Samuel to Saul, 1 Samuel 15:23.

4. He makes his fancy, his senses his gods; idolises them in seeking to please his fancy, his senses, rather than God. How common is this! When that preaching which is most pleasing to God will not please men, but that which most gratifies a vain, a wanton fancy; when men will displease God rather than displease their eye, in turning it from ensnaring objects; displease God rather than turn away their ear from filthy and unclean discourse; rather than not gratify a brutish sense, in lascivious gestures and wanton dalliance; rather displease God than put themselves to the trouble of making a covenant with their eyes, and keeping a strict watch over their senses: hereby you shew you had rather please your senses than please God. And what is this but to advance them into the place of God, and idolise them?

5. Others make their belly their god. Of this, Philippians 3:19; do more for their bellies than they do for God; care more what they shall eat or

drink, than how they shall serve or honour God; aim more at their own ease, and the commodities of this present life, than they regard God or the life to come; make it their end rather to provide for this than to provide for their souls. This is to serve their bellies instead of God. Such idolaters are epicures, whose language is, Let us eat and drink, etc.; life is short, therefore let us be merry while we live. Such idolaters are gluttons and drunkards. All inordinacy in this kind has a tincture of idolatry. Such idolaters are the poorer sort of people, who are immoderate in caring for the things of this life. The apostle thus explains this idolatry, when he adds, 'who mind earthly things,' etc. Such idolaters are the richer sort, when they will spend more on superfluities than they are willing to lay out for God, grudge to lay out so much for the refreshing the poor members of Christ, maintaining the gospel, or other religious uses, as they will ordinarily spend in a feast. Such are those who will offend God rather than not gratify their appetites. In a word, such are those who make it the main end of their callings, employments, endeavours, to provide for themselves plenty. This is to serve their bellies, not Christ, of which the apostle, Romans 6:8. And to serve this instead of God is to advance it into the place of God, to idolize it.

6. Some make their pleasures their God. Either sensual pleasures, of which before, or intellectual pleasures. Whatever the heart immoderately delights in, whether objects of

sense or objects of the mind, he makes it an idol. The apostle prophesies of such idolaters in the text, 2 Timothy 3:4. Thus men offend, not only in unlawful pleasures, but those that are indifferent. To instance in recreations; when men spend that time in recreations which should be spent in serving God, either in duties of general or particular callings, this is to serve themselves more than God, to be lovers of pleasure more than lovers of God.

7. Men make their credit their god, preferring their credit and repute in the world before the honour of God. This idolatrous humour was the cause why the Jews rejected the Son of God, John 5:44; 'They loved the praise of men,' John 12:43. This appears, when men will not endure a reproof for sin, though it proceed out of zeal to the glory of God; when they can better endure to hear and see God contradicted in the lives and words of men, than to have themselves crossed or contradicted in a word or deed; when they can more patiently see God dishonoured, than hear themselves disparaged; when it grieves not men so much to see Christ undervalued, neglected, as themselves slighted and disrespected; his word, ordinances, messengers, contemned, despised, as their own parts, judgments, disesteemed or disparaged; can pass by affronts, indignities offered to God, but their hearts rise against those who diminish their own reputation amongst men. When men make it more their aim to be well accounted of, well reported of in the world, than

that God be glorified, Christ advanced, and the gospel adorned, this is to prefer their own reputation before God's glory, and to idolize it. When men do their good actions to be seen of men, make a show of more outwardly than there is within, are more zealous, active, enlarged, in the view of the world than in secret, when God only sees; this shews they seek their own repute more than the honour of God, and so make it their idol, advancing it into the place of God.

8. Men make wealth and riches their god, when their hearts and minds are more set upon the things of the world than upon God. Then is this world idolized; and this the Scripture calls again and again idolatry. Nothing more evident and common, and yet nothing more difficult, than to convince men of their guilt herein. But if you will impartially answer these questions, you will see reason to suspect yourselves, and cry guilty, and bewail your guilt herein.

(1.) Do ye not value these things more than the light of God's countenance?

(2.) Do ye not love them more than holiness, than spiritual riches, the riches of Christ?

(3.) Do ye not desire the increase of them more than growth in grace?

(4.) Do ye not delight in them more than in communion with God, fellowship with Christ?

(5.) Do ye not grieve more for disappointments herein than God's with-drawings?

(6.) Are ye not more affected with worldly crosses than soul distempers?

(7.) Are ye not more afflicted with wants of these things than spiritual wants?

(8.) Are ye not more eager in seeking these than following after God?

(9.) Think ye not earthly enjoyments to be greater security than the great and precious promises?

(10.) Are not the thoughts of them more pleasing, welcome, than the thoughts of heaven and of Christ?

(11.) Do ye not esteem others more for these than for their interest in God?

(12.) Are not these your hope and confidence of security against an evil day?

(13.) Do not these employments make you omit holy duties, or cut them short, or perform them in a careless, heartless manner, hereby serving God as though ye served him not, as though ye cared not to enjoy him?

(14.) Do not your hearts stick so fast in this thick clay (as the prophet calls it), as you can scarce raise them towards God in prayer or heavenly thoughts?

(15.) Do ye prize these more, out of any other respect, than because hereby you may be most serviceable to God?

(16.) Are ye not more careful to increase or preserve them than to employ them to the utmost for God? If it be thus in any of these respects, much more if in all, it is too evident your hearts and minds are carried idolatrously after this world, it is too much your idol. You mistake if you think all is well, while you covet not that which is another's, or seek not to get them by unlawful means. If you be innocent herein, you may yet idolize the world in all the fore-mentioned respects, and many more than I can now mention. This may suffice to discover their sin, to those who are willing to know it.

9. Some make their relations their god, idolize husband, or wife, or children, by setting their affections more upon them than upon God; and this appears when they take more comfort in them, rejoice more in their company, than in the enjoyment of God; when they are more impatient of their absence than of God's departings, hiding or concealing himself from their soul; when more afflicted for the loss of them than for the loss of God's favour, in the comfortable sense and effects of it; when more fearful to part with them than to live at a distance from God; when more careful for their comfortable subsistence than that they may be serviceable to God. This is to prefer them before God, to idolize them.

10. Some make their friends and allies their god. When they rely more on them than on the Lord, they idolize them. Judah is charged for thus relying on Egypt, Isaiah 31:1, 3. When they depend upon these for counsel, advice, for help, assistance, for supplies or provisions, more than they rely on God for these, they are idolized.

When the heart is borne up with cheerfulness and confidence, while these outward dependences are afforded, but when they are removed, sinks into perplexities, discouraged, it appears in this case that these are more your confidence than God, that these are preferred.

11. Many make their enemies their god, when they fear man more than God, 1 Peter 3:14–15. When we fear him that can only kill the body, more than him who can cast both body and soul into hell, then God is not sanctified, *i. e.* he is not worshipped. That worship which is due unto God only is given unto man. When men are immoderately troubled, disquieted, perplexed at apprehensions of danger to their liberty, estates, lives, from men, not being so apprehensive of danger to their souls from the justice of God; when venture rather to provoke God than to provoke a man of power; when the wrath of a powerful enemy is more dreadful than the wrath of the almighty God; when ye are more startled at the threatenings of men than those threatenings that are denounced against sin by the word of God: then men are exalted above God, and our enemies are idolized.

12. Some make the creatures their god, so are guilty of idolatry (to waive other instances) when they swear by the creatures. Swearing, in Scripture, is frequently put for the worship of God, as being a special part of his worship. (And so it appears, what horrible profaneness it is, to swear by the name of God vainly, rashly, customarily, as many ungodly persons use to do in common discourse.) So it is used, Deuteronomy 10:20, Isaiah 19:18, for worship in the New

Testament, Isaiah 65:16, Jeremiah 12:16. We profess that to be our god by which we swear; for an oath is an invocation of God, as a witness of the truth sworn, and a punisher and avenger of falsehood. Now, invocation is a part of worship; and, therefore, when we swear by anything but God, we worship it as God, which is plain idolatry; hence that fearful expression which should strike terror into all guilty of such swearing, Jeremiah 5:7.

Thus it is idolatry to swear by the saints departed, by Mary or Peter; idolatry to swear by the rood or mass; a popish, idolatrous custom too common amongst us. This is to swear by the idol of the papists, and so to acknowledge it as our god. See how dreadfully the Lord threatens a sin just like this, Amos 8:14. Sin is the idol of Samaria, who, in their revolt from the true God, worshipped the God of Israel, in the similitude of the creatures set up in Dan and Bethel; as the papists do in other resemblances. Those that swear by this idol, the Lord threatens they shall fall, etc. And is it not as great a provocation to swear by the popish idol, the mass, the rood? It is idolatry to swear by the light, the heavens, fire, or other creatures; the sin of the Pharisees, for which Christ reproves them, Matthew 5:34. To swear by the name of God, as men do in common discourse, is high profaneness. To swear by any but God, is idolatry; for that by which ye swear, is worshipped as God only should be worshipped, and so idolized.

13. Men make Satan their god, giving that to him which is due only to God. Indeed, when any idol is set up, and worshipped with the soul, or with the body, then the devil is worshipped, 1 Corinthians 10:20; and what he speaks of the Gentiles, is spoken also of the Israelites, Deuteronomy 32:17; hence Jeroboam's idols are called devils, 2 Chronicles 11:15. It is like they intended to worship God in their idols; but, in the Lord's account, it is a worshipping of devils.

More especially, Satan is idolized, when men go to wizards, cunning men, as ye call them, such as are in covenant with the devil. This is forbidden, and joined with the abominable idolatry of Moloch, Leviticus 20:6; it is expressed by a phrase, by which the Lord uses to express idolatry, to 'go a whoring after.' This sin was Saul's ruin, 1 Chronicles 10:13–14. To inquire of these, is to inquire of the devil instead of God, and so to prefer him before God; horrid idolatry!

But this idolising of Satan is more common and universal than this consulting of wizards. Something of this idolatry is to be found almost in every sin; for then we idolize Satan, when we obey him rather than God; which appears when we yield to his suggestions and temptations rather than to the commands of God in his word, rather than to the motions of his Spirit in our hearts. This is to obey Satan, this is to serve the devil rather than God; and his servants ye are, whom ye obey; that is the apostle's rule. Now, by becoming his servants, you advance him into the place of God, giving him that service which is due only to God; and so he is called the god of this world, 2 Corinthians 4:4. Not that he is so, but because sinners, by serving and obeying him, by entertaining his suggestions, yielding to his temptations, do, in reference to this obedience, make him so. When Satan is obeyed rather than God (as he is in most, if not in every, sin), then he is preferred before God; and Satan is made the idol which you worship.

14. Men make their lusts their god, when they serve their lusts rather than God. As it is idolatry to serve and worship the creature more than the Creator, Romans 1:25, so it is idolatry, and much more abominable, to serve our lusts more than the Creator, these being the vilest things in earth or hell. There is a service due only to God, Matthew 4:10, and when we yield this service to our lusts, then we serve them as God only should be served, when we serve them absolutely. That this may be clear, observe there is a twofold service: 1, absolute, which is without reference and subordination to another, and this is due only to the God of heaven; 2, relative, when we do service to others, but in reference and subordination to God. Thus we may serve one another, as we are exhorted, Galatians 5:13. But this service of others must be in reference to God; we must serve them for God, as the apostle directs, Ephesians 6:7.

Now, we cannot serve our lusts, in reference to God, nor for his sake; these are quite opposite, no way subordinate; and therefore, if we serve our sin at all, we serve it absolutely, as God only should be served, which is plain idolatry. We cannot serve the Lord in serving our lusts; no man can serve these two masters; and therefore, so far as we serve sin, we are the servants of sin, not of God; it is our idol. So the apostle, Romans 6:16–17; that is your god which you thus serve; and, therefore, they serve divers gods, who serve divers lusts, Titus 3:3; Romans 6:12–13.

But when do men thus serve sin? Why, always, when they 'obey it in the lusts thereof;' when they obey their lusts rather than God; when they yield their members instruments of unrighteousness unto sin, rather than instruments of righteousness unto God; when yield to the motions of corrupt nature, rather than the commands of God. Then ye serve sin, as God only should be served. Examine, then, whether guilty.

When a worldly lust moves you to lay out your thoughts, endeavours, affections, upon the things of this world, and the Lord commands you to use the world as though you used it not, to rejoice, love, etc., which of these is obeyed?

When the flesh prompts you to uncleanness, intemperance, and that either speculative or actual; and the Lord commands ye to suppress these motions, and mortify the flesh: which of these is obeyed?

When corrupt nature moves you to revenge, to use means to come even with those that have wronged you; and the Lord commands you to love

your enemies, to return good for evil: which of
these do you obey?

When a proud, ambitious lust tempts you to
slight, undervalue others, to prefer yourselves
before them; and the Lord commands you to be
vile in your own eyes, to prefer others in honour
before yourselves: which do you obey? If these
lusts be obeyed before the Lord's commands,
you prefer your lusts before God, you shew yourselves servants of sin, rather than servants of
the God of heaven. You idolize, etc., when you
delight more in gratifying these lusts than in the
service of God. When you take more care, more
pains, to make provision for the flesh, to fulfil
the lusts thereof, than to comply with the will of
God, in using all means to mortify these lusts,
you serve your lusts rather than God; you render
that service which is due to God unto those lusts
that are viler than any toad or serpent; you make
your sin your God. And if it be thus, how common
then is this abominable sin of idolatry! how innu-
merable are those idols which men set up in the
stead of God! If, not only as the prophet upbraids
the Jews, 'according to the number of your cit-
ies,' Jeremiah 2:28, but according to the number
of your relations, of your senses and faculties,
nay, according to the number of your lusts, which
are as sand on the sea, etc., so are your gods.
O enter into your own hearts, search them out,
be ashamed of them; fly to Christ for pardon of
them, for strength against them. See here the
horrid sinfulness of a corrupt nature, how it

swarms with idols, how it is wholly idolatrous, and from hence see the necessity of a Saviour, of pardoning, mortifying, renewing grace.

2. We have searched out this idolatry by inquiring after those idols which are worshipped instead of God, let us search after it further by inquiring what acts of soul worship they are which are given to these idols. Hereby the guilt of this secret sin will be more fully discovered, and the examination tend more to conviction. These acts of worship are many. Examine,

1. What are your apprehensions. The Lord being infinitely and most transcendently glorious and excellent, he challenges our highest apprehensions, as due only to himself. If he be not in our judgments preferred above all things, he is not worshipped as God. Whatever is advanced above him, or equally with him, in our esteem that is idolized. Now because this in general will be denied, examine it by these particulars. *In generalibus latet dolus.*

(1.) What knowledge do ye most affect? The soul will be prying into that which it counts most excellent. The angels, 1 Peter. If ye be without the knowledge of God, if ye desire it not, Job 21:14. If ye study not this more than anything in the world, count it not most excellent, so as to count other things dross, Philippians 3. If ye can better be without this knowledge of God in Christ than without the knowledge of those things that concern your health, estate, repute in the world; if more industrious, etc.

(2.) What is it you would most appropriate to yourselves? What is it you most endeavour to make sure of? That which a man accounts most excellent, that he will labour to make most his own. Give ye all diligence to make sure your friends, your estates; and are you negligent to make sure your interest in God? Think ye no assurance too much there? and can ye be content to live at uncertainties, content yourselves with weak hopes and probabilities here? A sign, etc.

(3.) What is it you admire? Can you admire worldly excellencies, while the discoveries of Christ affect you little? Can you admire the parts, the achievements, the labours of others, while ye have low thoughts of God? Are ye better pleased to have yourselves admired than the Lord extolled? A sign God is not highest.

(4.) What do ye most praise? That will be most praised which you apprehend most excellent. Are ye much in the praises of God; often speaking such things of him to others as may endear him to them, as may raise their esteem of him? Take ye all occasion to speak great things of his name; or are ye much in the praising of men, means, instruments, little in praising God? Can ye rejoice more to hear yourselves praised, extolled, than ye do in praising God? A sign God is not praised as he ought.

(5.) What do ye glory in? That which ye count most excellent will be your glory. Do ye glory in your wealth or friends, in your parts or performances, in your wit or strength, in anything or

all together, as much as in God? Jeremiah 9:23–
24, Galatians 6:14.

(6.) What do ye value others for? Because
they are great, or wise, or rich, or powerful, or
fair? Do ye esteem them for anything more than
for their interest in God, or their resembling of
him? A sign God is not highest.

(7.) Are you willing to part with all for God?
A man will be ready to lose all rather than that
which he esteems more than all. He in the par-
able resolved to sell all he had, that he might
purchase the pearl of great price. Paul counted
all things loss, Philippians 3:8; the disciples
left all to follow Christ. If you be not willing to
part with riches, embrace poverty, when Christ
calls for it; part with relations, hate father and
mother; part with ease, accept of sufferings; part
with credit, welcome reproaches, for Christ's
sake; you have higher apprehensions of others. He that 'will not leave houses and lands,'
etc., Matthew 10:37, 'is not worthy of me.' Not
worthy, because he has not worthy thoughts of
him, prefers other things. So it is evident, when
men will part with Christ rather than their sins;
will not leave deceit, worldliness, intemperance,
uncleanness for Christ; Christ is undervalued,
these are idolized. The worship which is due only
to God you pay unto them; thus this idolatry will
be manifest by your apprehensions.

2. What are your thoughts? Much of the
inward worship of God consists in thoughts of
him. That which your mind is most set upon,

that which your thoughts are most taken up with, that you worship as God; where your treasure is, there will your hearts be also; that which your thoughts do chiefly run upon, that is most precious to you, that you ordinarily make your chief good. David was a man after God's own heart; why? His thoughts, his heart, ran most after God: 'My soul thirsteth for thee; I remember thee upon my bed, and meditate on thee in the nightwatches,' Psalm 63:6; 'I have set the Lord always before me,' Psalm 16:8; 'When I awake, I am still with thee,' Psalm 139:18; 'Yea, I am continually with thee,' Psalm 73:23. Hereby he shewed he had no other gods but the God of heaven, as he professes: 'Whom have I in heaven but thee? and there is none in earth that I desire besides thee,' verse 25. Hereby he manifested he was not in the number of those idolaters that are far from God, that go a-whoring from him, of whom he speaks, verse 27. Try by this if you are not in this number.

(1.) If you have any thoughts of God, are they not few and rare? Do ye not forget God? Are ye not unmindful of him whole days, whole nights together? Do not the thoughts of other things take up your hearts, and leave no room for thoughts of God, even when you are called to meditate on him? Are there not some, of whom for the most part we may say, God is not in all their thoughts; who live a great part of their days without God, without thoughts of God in the world? The mind is in the mean time employed, though God be not the object of it. That which is entertained when he is excluded, that takes place of God, is set up as an idol; and those thoughts which are due to God, are the idolatrous worship of this idol.

(2.) Are not thoughts of other things more pleasing, more welcome, than thoughts of God? find they not easier admission and freer entertainment? When the mind is right for God, it is of David's temper, Psalm 139:17–18. These were precious guests to David; so precious, he knew not sufficiently how to value them. And though they were more in number than the sands, yet did he not grudge them entertainment; they had free admission into his soul: 'Continually, night and day, I am still with thee.' He reckoned this amongst his chief treasures. Are not you of another temper? May ye not truly say, How precious are the thoughts of my worldly comforts and enjoyments to me! how sweet are the thoughts of revenge to me! how delightful are the thoughts of forbidden pleasures to me! whenas the thoughts of God, of glory, of Christ, of spiritual things, are a burden. By this you may know what god you serve; whether the world, your pleasures, your lusts, vanities, or the God of heaven. What thoughts fill you most with contentment and comfort? What are your greatest refreshment? If thoughts of God be most delightful, then you serve, you worship him; if thoughts of the world, etc., be most pleasing, most welcome, then you serve, you worship them, Psalm 94:19. What are the objects of those thoughts which are the comforts, the delight of your souls, etc.?

(3.) What thoughts are most abiding, most fixed? Are the thoughts of God passant and fleeting, when other thoughts make their abode with you? Do vain thoughts lodge within you, when thoughts of God and heavenly things give but a short visit, and away? Are these your inmates, dwell in your minds as at home; when those are but strangers, and have scarce encouragement to sit down, or make any stay in your souls? Why, then, it is suspicious, the objects of those thoughts that are so consistent are advanced into the place of God; they have that worship which is due only to the God of heaven.

3. What is your last end, your chief design? God being the chief good, should be the last end; and to be chiefly aimed at, most intended, as a principal act of soul-worship, due only unto God as the last end. Now, most men have other ends; God is not the last, the chief. But how shall this be known, since few or none will acknowledge it? It may be discerned by the effects and properties of the last end.

(1.) It excites the agent; *finis movet ad agendum*. It stirs up to actions, and may be assigned as the chief reason of our actings. Try, then, by this. You are in continual action and motion one way or other, what is it that sets you on work? what is the principle of your motion? why do you drudge and toil, take such care and pains, go to bed so late and rise so early? Is it that you may be great

or rich? is it that you may live in plenty or pleasure, and leave enough for posterity? Is this all?
or is this the chief motive that sets you a-work?
Why, then, God is not your end, other things are
advanced into his place. Otherwise your chief
motive would be, in all your cares, labours, that ye
might honour God, that ye might please him, that
your employment might be more serviceable to
him. These would be your aim above all, but that
other things are above God in your intentions.

(2.) It directs the agent; *dat ordinem mediis.*
If God be your end, you will be ordered by him, so
as to move to that first which is next to himself.
You would give that the pre-eminence which is
best, which is next to the last end. Try, then, by
this: do ye not prefer worldly employments before
spiritual, prayer, meditation, self-examination,
etc.? Do ye not seek riches, pleasures, more than
holiness? Do ye not neglect to seek the kingdom
of God and the righteousness thereof? Do ye
not mind the world more than your souls? Must
spiritual duties be content with the second place,
or no place at all? Would ye not omit a spiritual
duty rather than lose a worldly advantage? Is
not heaven less regarded than earthly things? If
thus, it is evident God is not your last end; something else takes place of him, is idolised, and
aimed at more than God. If the Lord, as the last
end, were your motive, director, you would move
first and most to those things, to those employments, that have most affinity with him, most
spiritual, most heavenly advantage.

(3.) It regulates the agent; limits him to those means only which serve to attain the end. He that makes riches his end, will not be prodigal or careless; for these tend not to promote his design, but are destructive to it. He that makes credit, honour his end, will not be seen to act those things which tend to his shame or reproach; his end restrains him from these; those means are only chosen which are subservient. So if it be your chief end to honour, please, enjoy God, you will not live in any known sin; for this is utterly inconsistent with, quite repugnant to, this end. Nothing dishonours, displeases, deprives of God but sin; those therefore that allow themselves in any evil way whatsoever, it is impossible God should be their end. It is evident they give this worship to something else besides the living God, and herein are idolaters.

(4.) It moderates the agent; *finis dat modum et mensuram mediis*. It prescribes bounds to the use of means, so as one shall not exclude another. If God were your end, if ye aimed at him above all, you would not be so eager after earthly things, and so lukewarm in holy duties. You would not be so industrious for your bodies, and so careless of your souls; you would not be so forward for outward advantages, and so backward for God. While it is thus, etc.

(5.) It facilitates; *finis dat amabilitatem mediis.* It makes the means lovely and pleasing which tend to advance it. If the Lord be your end, then the ways of God will be the ways of pleasantness. Then it will be your meat and drink to do his will. The duties of mortification will not seem so harsh and difficult. You would not be so backward to, so weary of, prayer, hearing, reading. Meditation of God and spiritual things would be delightful. Self-examination, communing with your hearts, would not be tedious. Strict and holy walking, watchfulness over your hearts and ways, would not be looked upon as your bondage. While it is otherwise, God is not your end, some other thing does displace him in your hearts, and is preferred before him.

(6.) It compensates the agent. When attained, it is counted a sufficient recompence for all the care, pains, labour taken in pursuing it. If the Lord be your end, whatever you get by your endeavours, nothing will quiet, will satisfy you, but the Lord himself. Suppose you get a competent estate by your industry in your callings; suppose you have compassed your designs in point of credit, or profit, or other outward advantage: if you rest in this as a sufficient recompence, it is a sign your chief aim was not God. For when he is your end, nothing will quiet you, except you enjoy more of God in the increase of your enjoyments. If when your endeavours succeed in the world, you say with him, 'Soul, take thy rest,' applaud yourselves in outward successes, rest here, look not beyond these outward things, though ye enjoy no more of God, though ye are hereby no more serviceable to him, though ye bring no more glory to him, then the Lord is not your last end, other things are more aimed at, more intended, and the worship due only to God is given to them. Thus you may discover this secret idolatry by your ends and designs.

He that makes Christ his chief aim, if at length he finds him whom his soul loveth, this quiets his heart, whatever he want, whatever he lose besides. He counts this a full recompence, for all his tears, prayers, inquiries, waitings, endeavours.

4. What are your supports? What do ye depend upon in troubles and perplexities, in fears and dangers, in wants and necessities? That which your souls rely on you worship as god. For soul dependence is an act of worship due only to God: Philippians 3, 'Worship God in the spirit.' They who have confidence in the flesh, worship not God in the spirit; they give this spiritual worship to something besides God. But since every one will be ready to disclaim this, and profess that their trust is in God, and him only, let this be examined in these severals.

(1.) Do ye not sometimes make bold to use unlawful means? Do ye not use some indirect course to compass your ends, to obtain your desires, or free you from trouble? Why do men step out of those callings wherein providence has disposed them? Why do they use unwarrantable practices in their callings, lie, deceive, oppress, dissemble? Why do they use lawful means unlawfully, immoderately? Why so eager upon worldly things, as to neglect God, heaven, their souls? Why? But because God is not their support; and when the soul is not stayed upon him, it relies upon something else idolatrously. This was Saul's sin; the apprehension of an apparent danger from the Philistines put him upon that which the Lord had forbidden, 1 Samuel 13. And for this the Lord cast him off. More inexcusable are they who use indirect courses, when they have no such temptation; who, to get a small advantage, will be unjust, unfaithful, unrighteous; care not to defraud others, so they may gain by it; come short of the heathens in point of true and just dealing. Nothing more evident than that the Lord is not your confidence, when ye use such practices. You idolize something else. Isaiah 28:16, 'Makes no haste.'

(2.) Do ye not seek less unto God, when your affairs are hopeful, prosperous, and means visible to accomplish your designs? Are ye not then less in prayer, not so frequent, not so instant, not so importunate, not so fervent in spirit? Are ye not more careless, more indifferent? This is a sign means and instruments are your support, rather than God. Where there is much confidence in God, there will be much seeking to him; for this is the vital act of confidence. Who is there, even amongst those who make conscience of seeking God constantly, that are not less in this duty, less hearty, zealous, enlarged, when their affairs prosper, and are like so to continue, than when they are in fears, danger? This argues the heart is something taken off from God, and stays more upon the creature.

(3.) Do not your hearts sink into perplexities and discouragements, when outward means fail, when your wanted supports are removed; when you are in want, and see none to relieve you as formerly; when you are in troubles, and see no means of deliverance; when you are in fears and dangers, and see no outward securities? Are your hearts then troubled, perplexed? Is such a condition too heavy for you? Can you not bear up cheerfully under it? Why, this argues those outward means now removed were more your support than God; otherwise he continuing still the same, your hearts would stay upon him, and find repose and security there, when all outward supports fail. So with David, Psalm 73:26; and the prophet, Habakkuk 3:17-19. This is the proper season for acting of faith, Isaiah 50:10.

5. What are your expectations? To expect that from other things which only is to be expected from God, is to give that to them which is only due unto God. Soul expectation is an act of inward worship, Psalm 62:5. Try by this. Do ye not expect heaven for your harmless carriage or good deeds? Do ye not expect pardon for your prayer, or mournings, or purposes not to sin? Do ye not expect your good duties will be accepted, merely because they are (as you think) well performed? Now what is this, but to expect from your performances what only should be expected from Christ? Do ye not expect contentment and satisfaction from the creatures, from outward comforts plentifully, peaceably enjoyed?

Whereas nothing can satisfy the soul of man but God only. Would ye not expect happiness from things below, if ye might enjoy them according to your hearts' desire? Is not this to expect from the world and outward enjoyment what only can be found in enjoying God? Do ye not expect your ends, merely because ye use the means, without looking further; expect knowledge, because you read or study; expect a competency in the world, because you are frugal, diligent, careful; expect your undertakings will succeed, because you manage your affairs with prudence, and follow your business with industry? Do ye not expect all these without looking to God for them? Oh no, every one will say, this will be universally disclaimed. Oh, but if you expect not these things but from God, why do not ye seek God for them? How is it that ye neglect prayer in your families, and when you go about your employments? How is it you do not frequently lift up your hearts to God, and send up your desires to heaven for success, for a blessing? How is it that you are so negligent in prayer, when you are diligent in using outward means? If ye did expect these things from God, you would seek to him heartily, constantly for them, and your hearts would be as busy, as diligent, as earnest in praying as you are in following your other business, Isaiah 36:37. Would your friend think you expect anything from him, if you never seek to him for it? Men's neglect of seeking God, or careless heartlessness in seeking him, shews plainly their expectations are more from something else than from God. Thus may you discover this secret idolatry by your expectations.

6. Where are your affections? Upon what do ye most fix them? That on which you most set your hearts and affections, that you worship as God. Examine, then, whether your affections be idolatrously placed more upon other things than God. Instance in love, fear.

(1.) What do ye most love? If ye love anything more than God, or equally with him, you are guilty of this idolatry. Idolatry is ordinarily called whoredom and adultery in Scripture. The apostle answerably calls those who immoderately love the things of the world, adulterers and adulteresses, James 4:4. Love of these things is idolatrous. She is an adulteress in soul who loves another more than her husband. So is he a soul adulterer, and so guilty of spiritual adultery, who loves anything more than God.

Oh, but you will say, God forbid that we should love anything more than God; he is not worthy to live that does not love God, love Christ, above all. This is generally taken for granted. Oh that it were not a general mistake! That we may not be deceived, try it thus.

[1.] Do ye love holiness above all other accomplishments in the world? Otherwise ye cannot love God above all things; for this is the image of God, the nearest resemblance of him upon earth. Now those that hate holiness, that scorn it under the names of puritanism, preciseness, they hate God indeed, whatever affection they pretend in word. Naturalists write of a beast that bears such an antipathy to a man, as he will tear and rend his picture. Those that manifest such antipathy to holiness, the image of God, do really hate God, however they disclaim it; and since they hate him, if they love anything in the world, they love it more than God.

[2.] Do ye love the people of God above all others? Those that are born of God are holy, strict, exemplary in their conversation. If these be not loved above others, others are loved more than God, 1 John 5:1, and 3:20. If these be the objects of your love, you will choose them before others for your companions; they will be the men of your counsel, of your delight, your eyes will be upon the faithful, Psalm 101:6, whereas vile, profane persons, you will avoid them; you will take no pleasure in their society. Those that hate, scorn, reproach, revile the people of God, inasmuch as they do it unto them, they do it unto God. They shew how they are affected unto Christ, by their disaffection to his members. If you hate these, represent them under what notion you please, you hate God; so far are ye from loving him above all others. Profane persons are the professed enemies of God; if you delight in their society, your hearts are joined to those whom the Lord hates, etc.

[3.] Do you hate sin, every evil way that ye know to be evil? Otherwise ye love not God at all, Psalm 97:10, Psalm 119:104. If ye delight in sin, willingly act it, live in it, notwithstanding the Lord forbids, threatens, hates it. Deceive not yourselves, if there be any truth in the word of God, the love of God is not in you. He that will not leave his sin for God, loves his sin better than God, idolizes it, gives that worship to his lusts which is due only to the God of heaven.

[4.] Do ye endeavour to obey Christ impartially? John 14:21, 23, 'If ye love me, keep my commandments.' He will do whatever he commands, how unpleasing soever it be to the flesh; how prejudicial soever it may prove to him in the world; however it cross his carnal humours and worldly interests; how inconsistent soever it be with his own ease, credit, advantage; how great, how small soever. He that lives in the neglect of any known duty, loves not God so much as that which moves him to neglect it. That has the pre-eminence, and is preferred before God.

[5.] How do ye bear the absence of Christ? Love is *affectus unionis;* it affects union, more of his presence, more intimacy, nearer enjoyment. Because he is most near in his ordinances, therefore he prizes, loves, longs for them; because he is nearer in heaven than in the ordinances, therefore he loves, longs, for the appearing of Christ. By this ye may know. Can ye not tell what it is to enjoy Christ, to be near him, to have communion with him? Can ye live contented at a distance from him, so be it you have but outward comforts in abundance? Can ye better endure the withdrawing of Christ than the absence of some endeared relation? Can you better dispense with the loss of his favour, in the comfortable sense of it, than the loss of wife, children, lands, goods? Would you offend Christ by sin, rather than suffer for him? Why, then other things have more of your love than Christ, and so are idolised. Thus discover idolatry by love.

(2.) Whom do ye most fear? There is so much of the worship of God in fear, as I told you, it is ordinarily put in Scripture for the whole worship of God. That which you most fear, that you worship as God; and if you fear anything more than God, you shew yourselves herein idolaters; but how shall it be discovered that we fear others more than God? Why, by these particulars:

[1.] Are ye not loath to reprove men for sin, lest ye should offend them? To admonish them when they offend God, lest ye should incur their displeasure? Do ye not connive, if not countenance it? Are ye not silent, if ye excuse not the sins of familiars, or others, lest by rebuking sin ye should exasperate the sinner against you? What is this, but to fear men more than God? When the fear of men is more powerful to hinder from performing that which God commands, than the fear of God is to move you to the practice of it, do ye not choose herein to offend God rather than man? more afraid to displease them than displease God?

[2.] Do ye not decline the profession of those truths, the practice of those duties, which profane men do jeer and scoff at, such as will expose you to their taunts and reproaches? What! be so strict, so precise, pray by the Spirit, repeat sermons, scruple at such and such small matters, play the dissembler! These are the reproaches of a profane world. Does the fear of this hinder you from any holy duty, from strict conscientious walking? Why, then you fear men more than God.

[3.] Are ye not more afraid to suffer than to sin? Do ye think it folly to be so scrupulous as to hazard your liberty, or estate, or life, rather than do what is unlawful? Would ye take liberty to sin rather than lose your liberty? strain your conscience rather than venture your estate? dispense with yourselves in omitting some known duty, or denying some truth, or admitting some unwarrantable practice, rather than endanger your life? Why, then, it is clear you fear something more than God. He that is not more afraid of sin than any loss or suffering whatsoever, is more afraid of something else than God, and so idolizes it.

[4.] Is not the threatenings of men more dreadful to you than the displeasure, the power, the threatenings of God? If men in power should send a pursuivant, and denounce to you, that in case ye are guilty of swearing, Sabbath-breaking, etc., he would see you put to death, and seize on your estate, would not this message daunt ye, startle ye, make ye tremble? Why, the God of heaven sends you many such messages. He has again and again threatened eternal death to

many sins that you are guilty of; yet you tremble
not, you little regard it. Is it not plain, then, that
you fear men more than God? Is not this such
idolatry as is here threatened with the loss of
heaven?

[5.] Are ye not more bold to sin in secret than
in the view of the world? Are ye not careful to
restrain sinful thoughts as well as scandalous
acts? Are ye not more fearful of such acts as the
law of the land will punish, than such as the
law of God condemns, such as are reserved for
the tribunal of Christ? Are ye not afraid to sin,
when no eye sees you but the eye of God? Do
not soul-sins, secret lusts, inward corruptions,
afflict and trouble ye? Why, then, it is apparent
you fear something else more than God. You give
that worship unto others which is due only to
God, which is the soul-idolatry here threatened.

7. Examine by your elections; what is your
soul's choice, when Christ and the world, Christ
and the flesh, come in competition? That which
you choose as the greatest good, that you make
your god. If you choose Christ, then the Lord is
your God; if you follow the flesh, embrace the
world, then these are your gods. This choice of
them, as the greater good, is that worship (and a
principal act of worship it is) due only unto God;
and when the flesh and the world carry it, they
are idolized.

These are the great competitors for the soul
of man, Christ, and the world, and flesh. That
interest which prevails, the soul bows down to it,

worships it as God should be worshipped. They are both importunate suitors, and offer great things to win the soul's consent; and that which it chooses it worships.

The flesh attempts the soul thus: If thou wilt follow me, live after my dictates and motions, close with my suggestions, make provision to satisfy me, then thou shalt live in ease and pleasure, gain many advantages in the world, avoid that trouble, those dangers, that persecution, that reproach and scorn, which the zealous followers of Christ cannot avoid.

Christ moves the soul thus: If thou wilt choose me, thou shalt have pardon, and peace, and life. 'He that findeth me, findeth life,' Proverbs 8:35. Thou shalt be freed from wrath, justice, hell; thou shalt have interest in all those glorious things that I have purchased with my blood. With such offers does Christ importune the soul in the gospel to accept of him.

Now, which of these prevails with you? Which of these offers seems best? Which motion do ye yield to? I know there are few or none but will be ready to say, it is Christ that I choose, I renounce the world and the flesh; the offers of Christ are gracious, and I have been always ready to yield thereto; God forbid that I should choose or prefer any thing before my Saviour! This is generally taken for granted; but, alas! it is generally mistaken, otherwise Christ's flock would not be so little, and those that are saved so few. Many suppose they choose Christ, while they embrace an idol. And this is the fatal mistake, the ruin even of most who enjoy the gospel. But how shall this be discerned? Why, Christ has discovered this clearly, if men were willing to see, if they had not rather be deceived than be at the trouble to examine by the rule. The soul that chooses Christ is willing to accept of him upon his own terms; this is the touchstone, etc. He that will not take Christ upon his own terms, his heart did yet never choose him. But what are Christ's terms? See Matthew 16:24. Now, do they deny themselves who will not deny a lust for Christ? Do men deny themselves, when self-love, self-seeking, self-pleasing, is so predominant, so visible? Do they take up the cross who lay it upon others? Are not they far from choosing to suffer for Christ rather than sin, who will sin when they are not tempted to it by fear of suffering? Do they follow Christ who walk contrary to him, who decline his ways as too strict, too precise; who brand zeal as madness, holiness as hypocrisy, circumspect walking as needless preciseness? Such do plainly refuse Christ, and choose their lusts and the world before him. That choice of Christ is only real and sincere, when the soul takes him, not only as a Saviour, but as a Lord. Try, then, by this. Are you as willing to be commanded by Christ, as to be saved by him—to submit to his laws, as to partake of his benefits? Do ye desire him as much to make you holy as to make you happy—as much for sanctification as for salvation—as much to free you from the

power sin as from the guilt of it—not only that
it may not damn you, but that it may not have
dominion over you? If you do not choose Christ
for this, and in this manner, you choose him not
at all. 'Tis plain, while you would have Christ for
your Saviour, something else is your god. The
interest of the flesh and world prevails, and this
you choose as a greater good in life, though ye
would be saved by Christ at death.

8. Examine by your inclinations. Your souls
are always in motion. Now, whither does this
motion chiefly tend, whither are they bound?
The inward worship of God does much consist in
the motion and inclination of the heart towards
God. When it moves most towards him, and but
to other things as helps and furtherances in the
way to him, then he is worshipped as God. But
when the heart moves more to other things than
to God, those things are idolised, and that worship is given to them which is due only unto God,
which is the idolatry we are now inquiring after.

Feel, then, the pulse of your souls; observe
their motion, that ye may know whether or no
it be idolatrous. Whither do the inclinations of
your hearts most carry you? Which way do they
most move, and to what objects? Do they move
most towards heaven or towards the earth?
towards Christ or sin? towards the enjoyment
of God, or towards outward enjoyments? towards
spiritual objects, grace and glory, holiness and
heavenly communion with Christ, or towards
carnal objects, your relations, sensual pleasures,

earthly advantages? If your hearts work more
after these, these are your idols, and these inclinations are idolatrous. The idolatry lies here in
the degree; it is lawful to move towards these
outward things; but when the heart is more carried after them than after God; when it is inordinate, then it is idolatrous. Now, that you may
discern in what degree your inclinations are,
observe these severals:—

(1.) Is your motion after God absolute, and
your inclinations to other things but subordinate and relative? Are your hearts carried after
these outward things for God? Move your hearts
towards them, that by the help of them you may
move faster after God? When your inclinations
are drawn out after relations, is it principally
because they have special interest in, or some
resemblance of, God? When you move towards
the world, is it principally that you may be more
serviceable to God in your generation? If not, you
idolise them. If your hearts move to these things
for themselves absolutely, and not in reference to
God, because they are like him, or because therein
you enjoy him, or because thereby ye may better
serve him; if not thus, your inclinations are idolatrous, your hearts hereby run a-whoring after
them, as the Scripture uses to express idolatry.

(2.) Are your inclinations after God stronger
than after other objects? Is there more life and
vigour in your motions heavenward? Are they
not more easy, more ordinarily, and with less
displacency, obstructed and diverted, than those

other things? Is the bent of your heart after God, when you are employed about worldly things? Is it not the affliction of your souls, that they move no faster, no more forcibly, towards Christ and glory, and that they are so easily turned aside to vanities? Can you say with David, 'My soul followeth hard after thee'? If your inclinations be strong to the world, your relations in it, employments or enjoyments in it, when weak and faint after God, these inclinations are idolatrous.

(3.) Are your inclinations after God more effectual than after other things? This will be discovered by your prayers, by your endeavours. The soul that moves effectually towards God breathes out many sighs and prayers and tears after him, is ever reaching at him, stretching out itself to meet him, to lay hold of him, to apprehend him. When he seems to withdraw, it follows him with strong cries and mournful complaints, 'How long, Lord, how long, etc.; O, when shall I come and appear before thee!' Now, then, if, when thou find not the comforting and quickening presence of God, yet, notwithstanding, you are still and silent in this sad condition, either pray not, or stir not up yourselves to pray with fervency, importunity, but content yourselves quietly in your ordinary way; why, then, it is evident your hearts are moving after something else more than God. So for your endeavours. If you can be diligent, careful, industrious in worldly business, but slack, negligent, careless in the ordinances, it is suspicious your inclinations are more after other things than God, which is idolatrous.

9. Examine by your fruitions. What is that in which you take most contentment, complacency, that which gives you most satisfaction? What is your sweetest and most delightful enjoyment, in which you rest best pleased? To delight in the Lord above all things is a special act of soul worship, due only unto God. When you delight in anything more, in anything so much as him, you give that worship due only to God unto other things, which is the idolatry here spoken of. If any enjoyment be more pleasing, satisfying, than the enjoyment of God, you erect an idol in the place of God. Examine: are not the ways of sin, intemperance, uncleanness, revenge, worldliness, more pleasing than the ways of holiness, wherein ye may walk with God and enjoy him? Do ye not more delight in earthly success, abundance, prosperity, than in the light of God's countenance, sense of his favour? Take ye not more contentment in worldly vanities than spiritual enjoyments? Take ye not more comfort in relations, wife, children, etc., than in communion with God and fellowship with Christ? Are not sensual pleasures more delightful than those which arise from spiritual and heavenly objects? Are not recreations or worldly employments more pleasing than those duties, exercises, wherein the Lord may be enjoyed? If they be, it is too evident the Lord is not your chief enjoyment. The heart is more taken, pleased, satisfied with something else than with God, which is to idolise it.

To examine this more punctually.

(1.) Can we rest satisfied without assurance of interest in God? Can we be content without the sense of his love? Can we be quiet in his absence? Are ye satisfied when ye find not the presence of God, the comfortable and powerful effects of it in your souls? Do ye rest in outward accommodations, health, plenty, friends, when ye have no certainty that the Lord is at peace with you? Do ye rest in the performance of spiritual duties, though ye find not the presence of God in them? Content with ordinances, though ye find not, enjoy not God in them? Why, then, God is not your chiefest enjoyment; something else does please you as well, if not content you better. You may see this in a familiar instance. The infant's most pleasing enjoyment is the breast; if it want this, nothing else will quiet it. Offer it heaps of pearl or mines of gold, nothing will content it without the breast. So it is with the soul that makes the Lord his chiefest enjoyment; nothing can content, quiet his heart, but the presence of God, the sense of his love, the power of his Spirit, the effects of his presence in his soul in spiritual light, life, strength, activeness, comfort. Outward comforts are unsavoury to him if he find not, enjoy not the Lord in them. The pleasures of the world are bitter to him while he misses his chief delight. He will sigh in the midst of others' mirth while the Lord, the joy of his soul, is removed. The ordinances themselves seem empty, when he sees them not filled

with the glory and power of the Lord's presence.
As she, 'What do all these avail me?' Give him
riches, or honours, or friends; let corn, and wine,
and oil increase; his heart is not quiet. What will
all these avail me if the Lord be absent, hide
his face? If you be satisfied with other things,
without regarding whether God be present or
no; contented though God be absent, though in
part withdrawn.

(2.) Are ye not backward to spiritual communion with God? more hardly drawn to those
duties, exercises, wherein ye may enjoy him,
than to some other enjoyments, some other
exercises in the world? Do not your hearts hang
back from secret prayer, meditation, exercise of
faith? Find you not yourselves much more forward to some other things? Oh, if the Lord were
your chief delight, your sweetest enjoyment, you
would be more eager, more forward to follow after
him. You need no enforcements; you go on your
own accord after the world, your relations, your
pleasures, recreations; and do ye need so many
motives, persuasions, inducements, enforcements, to draw you to God? Why, then, have ye
not cause to fear something else has more of your
hearts? The fruition of something else is sweeter
than that of God. This soul-worship is misplaced.

(3.) What cheerfulness find ye in drawing
near to God in those ways wherein he is to be
enjoyed? How cheerful are we when there, where
they most delight to be! How pleasant is the fruition of that which is their joy! Can you be thus

pleasant and cheerful in the company of friends, in the employments that tend to your advantage in the world, and yet so dull, untoward, heartless, in those services wherein ye may draw near to God, as though ye were cloyed with them? move here as if ye were out of your element; drive on heavily in these ways, as though the wheels were off, and come to these duties as to a meal with a full stomach? It is suspicious you delight in something more than God, give that worship to something else which is due only to God.

(4.) Are you not easily drawn from God? Are you not less discontented with a diversion from God than from some other things on which your hearts are set? That which you will easily part with, you are not much pleased with. Will not a temptation to take you off from close walking with God, prevail sooner than a motion to leave some sensual delight, ensnaring vanity? Can ye be more fixed and constant in other enjoyments and delights, but more easily, more ordinarily removed from God? This argues some distaste, some dislike of spiritual enjoyments. When the apprehension of such a pleasure, such an advantage, will be more powerful to turn ye aside from God than the promises of the word, the motions of the Spirit, and former experiences are to keep you close to him, this argues the Lord is not your most delightful enjoyment. Men do not easily part with that which is their chief delight; and if the Lord be not, something else is; and whatever that is, it is an idol.

(5.) Neglect ye not that which would make ye capable of the fullest enjoyment of God? Do ye not neglect holiness? Are ye not content with some low degrees of it? Is it your design, your endeavour to come up to the highest pitch of it? There is no seeing, no enjoying God without this. And the more of this, the more of God is seen, the more enjoyed. When this is in perfection, the enjoyment will be perfect. When this is weak, enjoyments will be small, and at a distance. The soul that counts the Lord his sweetest, most delightful enjoyment, will never think he has enough of him, and therefore will be ever labouring for that which will make him capable of more. If an opinion of holiness will serve your turn, or the beginnings, the principles of it, without the life, strength, exercise, increase of it, it is suspicious; you place not your happiness in the fruition of God; and if not in him, then it is in something else; and whatever that be, it is an idol.

Use 3. Exhortation. Be exhorted, in the fear of God, to avoid this idolatry. It is the apostle's exhortation, with which he closes his epistle, 1 John 5:21. Search it out, else how can it be avoided? Make use of the directions in the former use for that end at large delivered. If you discover it not, since such a discovery has been made thereof, it is because you will not see; and then henceforth this abominable sin in you is wilful, and yourselves inexcusable, and the justice of God clear, if any perish for it.

When you have found it, bewail it. Bewail it

with sorrow proportionable to the heinousness of the sin. Use it as an aggravation of your other sin, wherein, for the most part, there is a mixture. It may be thou art not an open blasphemer, an actual murderer, or a wretched apostate, but art thou not a soul idolater? Nay, there need no question be made of this. Go then in secret and blush before the Lord, and take shame to thyself, and be humbled for it, humbled deeply, for it is an high provocation.

Fly to Christ for pardon. O that this might be the issue of all delivered on this subject, to drive ye to Christ; not only to beget in you some slight ineffectual apprehensions of some need of a Saviour (with which too many content themselves to the ruin of their souls), but to possess you with deep apprehensions of an absolute necessity of him, of his blood. Nothing else can wash off the deep stain of this crimson sin. One act (though ye be guilty of millions) of this idolatry, will be enough to sink you into hell, enough to kindle the everlasting wrath of God against you; that wrath which will burn for ever, which will burn so as none can quench it, except the blood of Christ be applied to that purpose. See into what a sad condition this sin has already brought ye. Hereby,

1. You have forfeited an inheritance. It is not some parcel of your estate, some of less value, worth less consideration, but your inheritance, your whole inheritance, and that for ever. For a man to lose his whole inheritance is a great, a sad

loss; but this is it you lose by this sin. 'An idolater,' says the text, 'shall have *no* inheritance.'

2. Oh, but it may be the inheritance is little worth, and then no great matter if it be lost. Oh no; it is a rich, a large, a glorious inheritance you lose hereby; it is no less than a kingdom. The loss of a crown, the loss of a kingdom, sticks deep. Oh what hazards will not men run to save a kingdom! Their treasure, their blood, their lives, yea, and the lives of thousands, will men lose rather than lose a kingdom. Why, this is it you lose by this sin, no less than a kingdom. 'An idolater shall have no inheritance in the kingdom.'

3. Oh, but it may be it is some inconsiderable kingdom, some petty jurisdiction, then the loss is not so great. Oh no; it is the loss of the kingdom of God, and that is more than the loss of all the kingdoms of the earth. It is not the kingdom, the empire of a Cyrus, or of a Cæsar, or of an Alexander, or Othman, but it is the kingdom of God. You lose hereby such a kingdom as the empire of the world is but a span, a mote, yea, nothing, compared with it. Oh, what dreadful bloody conflicts there have been for the empire of the world! how many millions have been sacrificed to secure it! And will ye lose the kingdom of God rather than sacrifice this sin? The retaining of this sin will be the loss of that. So the text, 'An idolater shall have no inheritance in the kingdom of God.'

Oh, but though this loss, this hazard, be exceeding great, yet it may be avoided; though I continue in this sin, yet is there no hope in Christ? May not he admit me into this kingdom notwithstanding? Oh no; Christ has no kingdom for such; he never purchased a kingdom for those that will continue in this sin. Christ, who has made way for others to the kingdom, will himself shut soul-idolaters out of it. The text tells us this too, 'No inheritance in the kingdom of God, of Christ.'

Objection. But is this certain? Is this dreadful loss unavoidable? May it not be otherwise? Oh no; to dream of such a thing is madness; nothing is more certain. The apostle is in nothing more peremptory; mind the words, he says, 'An idolater shall not,' etc. He speaks not doubtfully, as of a thing uncertain, that may be or may not be. He says not, peradventure an idolater *may* not, but he *shall* not. As sure as the word of God is true, as sure as the apostle was directed by the Spirit of God, without all peradventure, a soul idolater shall have no inheritance, etc.

Objection. But is not this strange doctrine, to speak at this rate, of soul, of secret idolatry, a sin so common as few can acquit themselves of it; to say that all guilty of it shall certainly have no inheritance, etc. Is not this strange doctrine?

Answer. If it be strange, it is ignorance makes it so, for in the apostle's time it was a known, an acknowledged truth; there was no question, no doubt, made of it. The first word of the text tells us this, 'This ye know.' As if he had said, You certainly know, you undoubtedly acknowledge this; you make no question, no doubt of this, 'No idolater shall,' etc. No idolater, that is so habitually, perseveringly, shall. This idolatry, though it be secret, though it lodge in the retired chambers of the soul, though its pavilion be darkness, and no eye see it but the all-seeing eye of God, yet if it be not forsaken, lamented, resisted, subdued, it leaves no title, no way to the inheritance. Methinks this should be a sufficient dissuasive from this sin, a loss so great, so irreparable, so certain. This should effectually stir you up to search out this sin, to seek pardon of it, to get power to subdue it, to expel it. But further to stir you up against this sin, consider

2. How it is represented in Scripture, in what colours the Holy Ghost sets out idolatry.

(1.) It is called the worshipping of devils, not only in the Gentiles, 1 Corinthians 10:20, but also in the Jews, Deuteronomy 32:17. Yet these, in their idolatrous service, did not intend to worship devils, no, nor to worship their idols; but, as the papists pretend, to worship Jehovah, the true God, in those representations, as appears, Exodus [20:4?]. Now, what a horrible abomination is it to worship the devil! Samuel, when he would aggravate Saul's sin to the height, tells him it was like the sin of witchcraft and idolatry, these being the worst of sins. Yet, if we compare these, idolatry seems worse than witchcraft, for witchcraft is but a compact with the devil, but idolatry is a worshipping of the devil; now, is it not worse, a greater abomination, to worship than to make an agreement with him?

(2.) It is called whoredom and adultery, Judges 2:17; 'Went a-whoring,' etc., 2 Chronicles 21:13, Jeremiah 3:9; idolaters are called the 'children of whoredoms,' Hosea 2:4, and 4:12. It is spiritual adultery. The Lord can no more endure idolatry in his people, those that profess him, than a man can endure adultery in his wife; other failings may be borne with, but this calls for death or a divorce. Hence the Lord, where he forbids this sin, he adds this reason, Exodus 20. 'For I am a jealous God.' This provokes the Lord to jealousy; he will no more endure a competitor in his worship than a husband will endure a partner in the affections and enjoyment of his wife. He is a jealous God.

(3.) This is the principal character of antichrist. Babylon, the seat of antichristianism, is not called the tyrant of Babylon, nor the heretic of Babylon, but 'the whore of Babylon,' the mother of fornications and abominations, with whom the kings, nations, and kingdoms of the earth commit fornication, Revelation 17:5. Babylon,—mystery. It is a mysterious spiritual whoredom; her great abomination is whoredom in a mystery, opposite to the great mystery of godliness, the mystery of the true worship of God. Now, is it not a dangerous thing to have the least character, the least part of the mark of the beast, that mark by which the Lord has designed her and her partakers out to most dreadful and remarkable destruction?

(4.) The Lord does most severely, most

dreadfully threaten and punish idolatry above other sins. You may read the heinousness of it, in the grievousness of Israel's, of Judah's sufferings for it, Daniel 9:12. 'Under the whole heaven,' etc. The word confirmed hereby was the threatenings executed for this sin, than which the Lord threatened no sin more, none so much, by his servants the prophets. He punishes not only the idolaters themselves, but even their posterity to many generations after them, for this sin, according to the tenor of that threatening, Exodus 20:5; and the Jews are so apprehensive of it, as to this day they have a saying, That no judgment befel the Jews for those many hundred years after they left Egypt but there is an ounce of the golden calf in it.

Objection. But this was gross open idolatry, worshipping of images; it was not this secret, this soul idolatry; the Scripture speaks no such thing of that.

Answer. This secret and soul idolatry, is in some sense worse than open idolatry; and, therefore, those Scripture expressions setting forth the vileness and danger of that, may be applied to humble us under the sense of this. That this may appear, and mistakes may be prevented, remember wherein these two sorts of idolatry do consist. It is open gross idolatry when that outward worship, which consists in the gestures of body, bowing, prostration, etc., is given in a religious way to others besides God. It is secret idolatry, when that inward worship, which consists in the acts and motions of the mind and heart, are given to other things besides God. Now, when both inward and outward worship together are given to the creatures, that is the worst of idolatry of all; then the sin is complete in all the dimensions of its guilt. But now, if we compare these two sorts of worship apart, it is far worse idolatry, when inward worship is given to other things than God, than when outward worship only is communicated to them. And in this sense I say, that secret soul idolatry is worse than that which is gross and open, and that in divers respects.

1. The Lord more respects inward worship than outward, the acts and motions of the soul, than the acts and gestures of the body. 'My son, give me thy heart.' 'The true worshippers shall worship the Father in spirit,' John 4:28. It is inward, spiritual, soul worship, which the Lord most requires, most respects, most delights in, is most honoured by; and therefore it is a greater provocation to give this soul worship to other things than that of the body. It is worse idolatry for the soul to bow down to a lust, than for the body to lie prostrate before an idol.

2. Even in worshipping God, a man may be excessive in outward acts and expressions, in the motions and gestures of the body; but there can be no excess in the inward acts of worship. Ye cannot love God too much, nor trust, fear, desire, delight, nor have too much esteem of him, and this argues a greater excellency in, a

greater necessity of this inward worship, than of
that which is outward, and therefore a greater
provocation to give that soul-worship unto others, than this of the body.

3. The objects of secret idolatry are worse
than those of open idolatry, the idols worshipped
are more vile, more abominable; and, therefore,
the idolatry more to be abhorred. For the idols
here worshipped, the objects of soul-worship in
this secret idolatry, are for the most part the
lusts of men. Now, there is not the basest creature that ever the blindest of the heathen worshipped, that is so vile as our base lusts. There is
no creature so mean (not such as the Egyptians
worshipped) but has some goodness in it, Genesis
1, something of worth or use as it is a creature;
but there is no goodness at all in the lusts of men,
nothing but what is altogether and upon every
account most abominable, and that in the eye
of God, who judges of things as they are, and so
judges righteous judgment. He looked upon all
that he had made as good, even the meanest of
his creatures; but he cannot endure to look upon
men's lusts, he is of purer eyes than to behold
iniquity; so vile, so loathsome, so abominable,
so full of provocation, he cannot look upon them
but with indignation. Now for men to give that
divine honour, that soul worship which is due
only unto the Majesty of heaven, unto their vile
abominable lusts, must needs be more heinous,
more intolerable, than if it were given to the
works of God's hands, than if it were given to

the sun or moon, yea, or to wood and stone, yea, or to toads and serpents; for these are better, have more worth in them than our lusts, for they are the works of God's hands; whereas your lusts are the loathsome issue of filthy impure hearts.

When your lusts have more of your hearts, thoughts, delight, desires, love than God, it is worse idolatry upon this account than if you should bow to a sun or moon, than if you should lie prostrate before a toad or serpent.

Objection. But some may say, If we did make vows or prayers, if we did burn incense, or offer sacrifice to our lusts, then might we be charged with this idolatry; otherwise the censure seems to want good ground.

Answer. I have instanced at large in many acts of worship besides these, which are due only to God; and it is idolatry to give any one, not only these. But as for this objected, see if there be not something answerable to these, nay, something exceeding these acts of worship given by men to their lusts.

1. As for prayer and invocation. If the desires of your hearts be more after the fulfilling of your lusts, and making provision for them, than after the pleasing and honouring of God, why then, you pray more to your lusts than unto God. For if the desires of your souls be not after God, as they cannot be while your lusts prevail, why, then, that which you count praying to God is but the carcase of a prayer. Your lusts have that which is the soul and life of prayer. For the essence of

prayer consists in the ardent desires of the heart, the expressions and gestures are but formalities and circumstances, not at all regarded by God except in displeasure, when the other is absent, Isaiah 29:13. This was no praying; but Hannah's was without expressions, 1 Samuel 1:13, 15.

2. As for vows. If you purpose and resolve to live in sin, and follow the motions of your lusts, is not this a mental vow? This is equivalent to, and has the strength and firmness of, a vow, and is stronger than any resolution for God can be, while the strength of sin is unsubdued.

3. As for sacrifices. If you give up yourselves to any way of sin, you sacrifice more thereto than the cattle of a thousand hills. A man given up to a lust, he sacrifices his time, his strength, his enjoyments, his parts, his endeavours, his thoughts, his affections, nay, his soul thereto. And are not these more valuable than the sacrifices of bulls or goats? than any sacrifice of that nature in use among the Jews or Gentiles, Psalm 51:16–17. An heart broken, i. e. subdued to God, ready to yield to his will in all things, is a sacrifice to God. So is a heart subdued to a lust, ready to yield to its motions, it is a sacrifice to it; such a sacrifice as God requires for himself, and would be well-pleased with it, if it were offered to him; better pleased than with all external sacrifices.

Objection. But what does this concern the people of God already in covenant? Though they may be guilty of some inordinate, i. e. idolatrous motions, yet are not they hereby brought within the compass of this threatening. They cannot lose their title to the inheritance, that which they were ordained to, that which they are born to. 'The foundation of God standeth sure,' etc. 'Whom he has predestinated,' etc.

Answer. Be it so. They fall not directly under the threatening; yet does it sometimes concern them. If it did not, yet are there other weighty considerations that should make this sin dreadful even to God's people.

1. Though it make not their possession of the inheritance impossible, yet will this make it exceeding difficult. The apostle gives direction, 2 Peter 1:11, how an entrance may be ministered abundantly into the everlasting kingdom. Though the people of God, giving way to these motions, may possibly have an entrance, yet not abundantly ministered. It is one thing for a man to creep into his inheritance; another to be carried with full sail into it. The apostles speak of some that shall be saved, but so as by fire, 1 Corinthians 13:15; though they may escape this threatening, yet very hardly, with much danger and difficulty; even as out of the fire he shall be, מצל מאש, as a firebrand. The Lord Christ makes it such a difficulty as is next to an impossibility, Mark 10:23, etc. Now to prevent a mistake, he tells them, it is not the having, the possessing of riches, but the idolizing of them, trusting in them, ascribing that to them which is due only to God; which makes it thus exceeding difficult for those that have riches, etc. And there is the same

reason of all other things inordinately affected. He that inordinately loves, fears, delights, desires, esteems anything in the world, it will be exceeding difficult for such a one to enter. And lest any should make light of it, he further expresses the difficulty by a comparison, verse 25. There is but the difference of a letter betwixt κάμηλος, a *camel*, and κάμιλος, a *cable*; and this latter way some render it, 'It is easier for a cable,' etc. Take it which way you will, it speaks a difficulty impossible to be overcome by the power of man. And so he explains it, to allay the disciples' astonishment, verses 26–27. It is possible only to almighty power, which alone can so disengage the heart from riches and other objects, as it shall not immoderately affect them, inordinately love, desire, prize. There is no other way possible to heaven, but by subduing this idolatrous humour of trusting in, idolizing of, riches. And the same is true of any other object whereon the mind, the heart, is more set than upon God: 'It is as easy,' etc.

If you give way to these inordinate motions, affections, etc., you will find the way to heaven, like the Israelites' way to Canaan, tedious, difficult, dangerous. It was idolatry made it so to them. The Lord might have brought them a short, a safe, an easy way, to the promised land, and made it a journey of as few days as it was years; but their idolatry, with other sins, provoked the Lord to swear in his wrath, etc. And this very thing, both sin and punishment, is proposed as ensamples to us, lest, being ensnared in their sin, we should fall by their punishment, fall in the wilderness, and come short of Canaan, 1 Corinthians 10:6–7, 11–12. If this shut not the people of God out of his rest, yet it may make your way thither exceeding woful and perilous, exceeding difficult and hazardous; it may bring ye back into the wilderness, when ye are in sight of the land of promise; may dash your hopes, darken your evidence, and make your way on earth a dry and comfortless desert, a perilous and howling wilderness.

2. This will blast the prosperity of your souls, endanger the life of holiness, keep ye back from the power of godliness, bring your souls into a consumption, keep them in a languishing condition, even near unto the gates of death. And what greater miseries can befall a servant of God in this world? Oh, if we could look upon things with a spiritual eye, these distempers would be more dreadful than outward sufferings. When anything in the world is inordinately, *i. e.* idolatrously minded and affected, it is a soul disease, like to those diseases of the body which draw all the spirits and nutriment to the distempered part, and leave the rest weak and languishing in a consumption. While ye love other things inordinately, you lose your first love to Christ; while ye are so eager after the world and other vanities, you must needs be lukewarm in the ways of God; while ye are so active after a soul-idol, you cannot but be barren and unfruitful towards

God. And how dangerous are these distempers, how odious to the Lord, how severely does he threaten them!

This idolatrous plant will suck away all the juice and sap of your souls, and leave grace to wither and languish. It cumbers the ground wherever it takes place, and makes all about it barren.

There is no coming up to the power of godliness, to the vigorous exercise of grace, to the lively actings of holiness, no access to intimate communion with God, where this is tolerated. And what is the life of a Christian without this, but a shadow of death? If the hearts of lukewarm, formal, backsliding professors (who abound everywhere) were searched, some such imposthume would be found there, some lust or vanity idolatrously affected, imposthumating their hearts, and eating as a cancer; nor can our souls ever prosper, but will still be backsliding, till the ulcer be lanced. And are not such distempers dreadful, which bring the soul so near to apostasy? Should not this be a forcible motive?

3. If you continue in this guilt, you may be sure some sharp affliction will befall you. If the Lord have any love to you, he will not lose you: 'As many as I love, I chasten,' Revelation 3. Either he will pluck that from you which ye immoderately value and affect, or else he will so embitter it to you as you shall find by sad experience that it is an evil thing and a bitter that thou hast forsaken the Lord thy God, to set up other things instead of him, Jeremiah 2:19. He will make this very

wickedness to correct thee, and thy backsliding hereby occasioned to reprove thee; he will turn those idolized comforts into gall and wormwood, and convey a sting into that which thy heart, with such delight, embraces. If thou fall not in the wilderness (as habitual idolaters), yet will he turn thy idols into serpents; so that instead of the comforts thou expectest to refresh thee, thou shalt find a sting to wound thee. The Israelites' sufferings for idolatry and other evils are proposed as ensamples to the people of God, 1 Corinthians 10. If thou expectest to enjoy thy idol quietly, thou art deluded; if thou belong to God, he will make thee smart for it. If you will not speedily put away these spiritual whoredoms out of your sight, the Lord will strip ye naked, and make ye as a wilderness, Hosea 2:3; see chapter 5:6–7.

4. The Lord will withdraw himself from you. There must needs be an eclipse when the earth gets betwixt you and the sun. You will find the light of his countenance clouded when such gross vapours, such lusts, such inordinate motions abound. The Lord is a jealous God; if he do not send you a bill of divorce, yet ye shall have little of his presence; he will be separated in part, though not totally and for ever. And oh how sad will your condition be, if outward afflictions and spiritual desertions should meet together! If the Lord, for your idolizing the things of the world, should leave you destitute of them; if ye should fall into poverty, disgrace; if cast off by friends and relations, too much valued; if he should cast

you into languishing sickness, and then wound your conscience, drop bitterness into your spirits, and set his terrors in array against you; if you should cry to him in this condition, and he refuse to hear you; if seek him, and he not be found of you; if he should send you to the gods that ye have served; if he should bring to remembrance your idols, your credit, riches, pleasures, sports, company, relations, and say to you, as to them, Judges 10:13–14, Go and cry to these idols that you preferred before me, let them deliver you, let them speak peace to you, let them save you, let them free you from the wrath to come, let them secure you from going down into the pit. You have slighted, undervalued, cast off me when you prospered; and do ye come now to me when ye are afflicted? Nay, go to the gods that ye have chosen. You thought them more worthy of your thoughts, affections, hearts, than me; make much of your choice, eat the fruits of your doings, I will have nothing to do with you: Oh what a dreadful condition will this be? There is but even a span betwixt hell and it. Now, by continuing under this guilt, you are in the high way to this woful condition, you are posting towards it. Oh remember it before it be too late.

Question. But since this soul idolatry is so dangerous to all sorts, how shall it be avoided? What means may we use, to escape out of this dangerous snare?

Answer. For satisfaction to this, observe these directions.

1. Get new natures. All other means will be ineffectual without this. The regeneration of the soul is the only way to the destruction of this sin. The first beginnings of spiritual life, are the first pangs of death to soul idolatry; and as grace increases, as holiness grows, so does this sin decay. It ceases to be habitual and reigning, when the principles of grace are first implanted; and as holiness, which is Christ's interest in the soul, grows stronger and stronger, so the interest of the flesh and world, wherein the life and power of this sin consists, grows weaker and weaker. They are as the house of David and Saul. This is the woful misery of an unrenewed condition; and oh that it might be laid to heart by those whom it concerns! While ye are in the state of nature, unconverted, not sanctified, not born again, you are unavoidably idolaters. It is reigning and habitual, and so damning, and destructive, till ye be regenerated. Sin has the throne, Satan has the sceptre, every base lust and vanity takes place of God, of Christ, in your hearts. Whatever ye love, ye love it more than God. Whatever ye trust, delight in, desire, esteem, the god of this world is your god, and the lust of the flesh, eye, pride of life, is your trinity. God has no place in your minds and hearts, or but an inferior place, a place unworthy of him, below your lusts, vanities, relations, enjoyments. God has no true worship from you; that which is due to him is given to other things; and so it will be till you have new hearts, till old things pass away. Oh what

a woful condition is this! Be convinced of it. Cry unto God for the spirit of regeneration, for those new hearts which he has promised. Till then, you are, you will be, such idolaters as have no inheritance in the kingdom.

2. Mortify your lusts. It is the apostle's direction, Colossians 3:5. If we inquire, as the apostle James in another case, from whence comes this soul idolatry? we may answer, as he, James 4:1, 'Comes it not hence, even of your lusts that war in your members?' Here is the spring-head of this abomination. Stop up this, and the motions, the streams thereof will fail. When Delilah would destroy Samson, she inquired wherein his strength lay. Why, the strength of this idolatry lies in unmortified lusts; except ye cut these off, ye will never prevail against it. Oh that instead of those vanities, to which Satan diverts so many professors from the great concernments of their souls, this might be your care, and study, and design, to die daily. Be much in mortifying duties: 1, Search out your lusts, get more acquaintance with the distempers of your hearts; 2, Be ashamed of them; 3, Acknowledge them, with all their aggravations, be humbled for them in the sight of God, frequently, seriously; 4, Cut off the occasions which nourish, support them; 5, Beat down your bodies, and bring them into subjection; rather forbear lawful liberties, than yield any encouragement to your lusts by them; 6, Cry unto God for strength against this great multitude; look on them as more dreadful than an host

of armed enemies; as more dangerous, more per-
nicious; say as Jehoshaphat, 2 Chronicles 20:12;
7, Bewail them as your greatest afflictions; 8, Act
faith on Christ crucified, and by the power of it
draw crucifying virtue from him; it is through
his strength only that you must conquer. The life
of this sin is bound up in the life of unmortified
lusts. Crucify these, die daily unto them, and
this sin will die, will fall with them.

3. Get right apprehensions of the things of
the world. An overvaluing of outward things
is the birth and food of this soul-idolatry. The
motions and affections of the soul follow the dic-
tate, the judgment of the understanding; if this
be corrupt, no wonder if they be inordinate. The
judgment is the spring of the soul's motion; if
that be out of order, no wonder if all the motions
of the heart be irregular. Whence is it that we
immoderately love, desire, delight, trust, outward things, but because we overvalue them,
apprehend more in them than there is? Let
your thoughts often represent to your souls the
vanity, emptiness, uncertainty, dissatisfaction,
deceitfulness, unprofitableness of your choicest
worldly enjoyments, and the vexation of spirit
that attends them, and converse in the world
under the sense of these apprehensions. Look
upon them, as the Spirit of God represents them,
nay, as experience testifies of them, and the
ground of idolizing them will be far less. Consult
with the best experience, and stand to its verdict.
What did Samson or Solomon find in beauty, or

Haman in honours, or Judas in his money, or the
rich man in his full barns and exceeding plenty,
or David in his dearest child, or Job in the wife
of his bosom and choicest friends? Oh miserable comforts, miserable comforters! Are such
things worthy to come in competition with God?
Think seriously of these things, judge of them
as they are, use them as though ye used them
not. When you are crucified to the world, then
will this sin languish, then will the strength of
it be weakened.

4. Let your hearts be especially jealous of
lawful comforts; these are the most dangerous
snares. Because we apprehend least danger in
them, herein we are most secure, and therefore
the sooner surprised. Because we may lawfully
follow our callings and worldly business, therefore men take liberty to follow them too eagerly,
engage their minds and hearts too far upon
them, and that before they are aware of it.

Because we may lawfully love friends and
relations, we are less watchful to avoid excess
in our affections. Because recreations are lawful, therefore we are apt to take liberty to exceed
therein. Because we may take comfort in outward enjoyments, therefore we are more apt to
let out our hearts to them, as if they were our
chief comforts; especially when our employments
border upon spiritual things, we are apt to think
we cannot be too inordinate, whereas spiritual
things themselves may be carnally used. And
the extreme here is more easy to them that are

conscientious, than in things apparently evil. Oh, how many who escape the gross pollutions of the world, and are far from excess of riot, are miserably ensnared in the inordinate using and affecting of lawful things! Here we lie most open to Satan; therefore, if ye would avoid this idolatry, be most watchful and jealous in these things.

Printed in Great Britain
by Amazon

37047657R00057